SAN DIEGO PUBLIC LIBRARY

**ALWAYS BRING YOUR
CARD WITH YOU.**

The Impossible Observer

The "Impossible Observer

Reason and the Reader in 18th-Century Prose

Robert W. Uphaus

THE UNIVERSITY PRESS OF KENTUCKY
Lexington   c 1979

Library of Congress Cataloging in Publication Data
Uphaus, Robert W
    The impossible observer.

    Includes bibliographical references and index.
    1. English prose literature—18th century—
History and criticism. I. Title.
    PR769.U6   820'.9'006   79-4014
    ISBN 0-8131-1389-X

Scholarly publisher for the Commonwealth,
serving Berea College, Centre College of Kentucky,
Eastern Kentucky University, The Filson Club,
Georgetown College, Kentucky Historical Society,
Kentucky State University, Morehead State University,
Murray State University, Northern Kentucky University,
Transylvania University, University of Kentucky,
University of Louisville, and Western Kentucky University.

Editorial and Sales Offices: Lexington, Kentucky 40506

For my mother

Contents

Acknowledgments

While writing this book I have incurred many debts. I am especially grateful to Professor David Vieth who has followed my book at almost every stage of the way, and whose persistent efforts in my behalf I shall never forget. My wife, Sue, has applied her customary editorial skill to my book. I also wish to thank the editors of *Papers on Language and Literature*, *Studies in Burke and His Time*, and *Studies in the Novel* for allowing me to reprint portions of my book, and I would like to acknowledge the financial help I have received from both the College of Arts and Letters and the All University Research Fund at Michigan State University.

1
The Impossible Observer

Any adequate critical system must take into account its own assumptions, expectations, and operations regarding four discrete matters: (1) the reader's experience of texts, (2) what constitutes a literary text, (3) the manner in which literary meaning is determined, and (4) the relation of criticism as a distinctly literary activity to the reader's larger assumptions concerning human nature. Although any one of the four enumerated subjects may receive within specific critical systems more emphasis than the others, the foundation, if not the center, of any critical system is inescapably the reader. Criticism does not write itself; literary texts do not make themselves; meaning does not create itself.

While it is a truism, if not a cliché, that all the activities associated with criticism radiate outward from, and therefore assume, a reader, few critical systems take this fact into account. The reason for such silence is not hard to find; for it is still the dominant view of many critical systems that real, which is to say demonstrable and verifiable, knowledge derives only from the ability to contemplate facts "objectively." And if there is one thing, so the assumption goes, that does not lend itself readily to objectivity, it is the reader, who is by definition something wholly subjective. Now the assumption of objectivity in literary criticism largely derives from the wish on the part of many critics to approach literary meaning as if it conformed to certain laws of literature (concepts of genre, for example) which could be verified by means similar to the empirical procedures associated with scientific method. Such an approach is conspicuously represented both in Northrop Frye's *Anatomy of Criticism*, which treats literature as a closed system, and in E. D. Hirsch's *Validity in Interpretation*, which assumes at the outset a distinction between meaning—something stable, intended, and verifiable—and significance—something indeterminate, associational, and ultimately personal.

In this book, however, I shall argue that some of the principal texts of eighteenth-century English literature elicit their meaning by deliberately juxtaposing the expectations of rationality, objectivity, and aesthetic closure against the larger and more problematical experiences of reading about, and imaginatively identifying with, characters and situations which are continually human though not consistently determinate. Many eighteenth-century texts do not reinforce the expectations of "objective" criticism so much as they challenge the reader into a new or renewed awareness of just how problematical the nature and formation of all beliefs, assumptions, expectations, and value judgments are. Many eighteenth-century texts, for example, do not reaffirm the customary expectation of finding meaning in the text, meaning which is ordinarily assumed to be governed by prior literary conventions that reinforce the expectations of order, stability, and objectivity. Though I do not intend to throw aside the customary interpretive activities of criticism, nor the reader's intellectual appreciation of literature, I do wish to emphasize, because they are so often ignored, those literary experiences that enlarge, encourage, and evoke the reader's active participation in literature, rather than his detached observation of what are abstractly called themes.

Lest my reader charge me with being arrogantly solipsistic and unhistorical, let me say that there is considerable precedent for my essentially affective approach to eighteenth-century prose. A good deal of scholarship has been devoted to the uses of rhetoric in eighteenth-century poetry and prose, especially satire; and rhetoric, as one can easily see in satire, is designed to affect specific audiences. There is no real point in my arguing that numerous writers in the eighteenth century were incredibly sophisticated about the theory and practice of rhetoric. While it is not my intention, nor perhaps within my ability, to give a detailed history of the influence of Cicero and Quintilian in English criticism from 1660 to 1800, it was surely a standard idea of this period that the purpose of the poet, like that of the Ciceronian *rhetor*, was to manipulate the responses of his audience. This interest in the affective dimensions of literature is evident in Addison's *The Pleasures of the Imagination*, about which Lee Elioseff has observed, "The problems raised by many of Addison's essays, especially those on *The Pleasures of the Imagination*, are those of a distinctly 'modern' psychological critic whose immediate concern is the effect of literature upon its audience." [1] Such a concern with affective literary theory, whose origins Elioseff suggests "are to be found in the late seventeenth and early eighteenth centuries" (p. 10), also derives from a Longinian interest in the sublime, so well documented by Samuel Holt Monk. Moreover, there is a conspicuous habit in much seventeenth- and eighteenth-century critical theory, running from Dryden to Reynolds, to use particular artistic figures from past and present as representative of either an Aristotelian emphasis on aesthetic order and imitation or a Longinian emphasis on aesthetic energy and invention. This recurrent contrast is evident in the frequent comparisons of Virgil and Homer, Horace and Juvenal, Ben Jonson and Shakespeare, Pope and Dryden, Fielding and Richardson, and even in Reynolds's later comparison of Raphael and Michelangelo. I am certainly not trying to suggest a monolithic construct, in which all these comparisons are alleged to be the same; but I am suggesting that they are a revealing habit of mind—one calculated to distinguish between an Aristotelian interest in aesthetic form and a Longinian interest in psychological effect.

This affective appeal is precisely what Edmund Burke calls attention to when he remarks, "In reality poetry and rhetoric do not succeed in exact description so well as painting does; their business is to affect rather by sympathy than imitation; to display rather the effect of things on the mind of the speaker, or of others, than to present a clear idea of the things themselves. . . . We yield to sympathy what we refuse to description." [2] What is far less attended to, however, is the way that such rhetorical sophistication translates into a kind of narrative which is avowedly affective and problematical, and which so often anticipates and revises the orderly expectations of objective criticism. Sir Joshua Reynolds can write, "Reason, without doubt, must ultimately determine every thing; at this minute it is required to inform us when that very reason is to give way to feeling," [3] but he continues to be thought of as the prototypical "Neoclassical" aesthetician. Samuel Johnson, whose critical system I will examine in other parts of this book, can write "there is always an appeal open from criticism to nature," [4] and he can tell us about both reading and living that "in estimating the pain or pleasure of any particular state, every man, indeed, draws his decisions from his own breast, and cannot with certainty determine, whether other minds are affected by the same causes in the same manner. Yet by this criterion we must be content to judge, because no other can be obtained." [5] Yet despite these and many other statements, relatively little attention—only Walter Jackson Bate's *The*

Achievement of Samuel Johnson and Jean Hagstrum's *Samuel Johnson's Literary Criticism* come easily to mind—has been paid to the
affective basis of Johnson's practice as a writer and a critic, and to his
demolition of the criterion of objectivity.[6]

A recent article, on the subject of modern physics, outlines an
approach that largely conditions the critical procedures of my study.
Interestingly, it is a modern scientist who dismisses the very idea of
an objective observer which dominates so much critical practice.
Richard Schlegel writes:

We have learned that man cannot describe the physical world as if his own
investigations had no effect upon it. The classical physicist who could sit, as
it were, on one side of a translucent screen with his thoughts and experiences,
viewing the world he studied on the other, is now the impossible spectator.
For much of physics the dividing screen is lost, and cannot be replaced . . .
the scientist now finds that he in fact has a role in the creation of the world
that he is describing. It is not, I should hasten to add, that his emotions bias
his results, but rather that his act of observation participates in forming the
natural world.[7]

Schlegel later speaks of demolishing the idea of "the detached spectator
who has no role in the determination of that which he sees," and this
idea of dismissing the "detached spectator" is precisely the basis on
which I have selected the texts whose affective appeal I shall examine.

Eric Rothstein has, from another angle, addressed himself to what
Schlegel has called the "detached spectator." In his recent article,
"'Ideal Presence' and the 'Non Finito' in Eighteenth-Century Aesthetics," Rothstein has forcefully questioned the notion that "in the eighteenth century the perceiving mind was a passive lackey for the absolut-
ism of the objective eye." Using Lord Kames's term "ideal presence"
to denote the reader's "imaginative expansion of the text," Rothstein
goes on to show how this ideal presence, or what might be called a
"subjective corollary," entails a "degree of indeterminacy" which is
necessary to the full realization of a literary text. Furthermore, Rothstein argues that "the doctrine of ideal presence urges the reader toward
deeply personal and yet fundamentally shared imaginative expansions,
which create a bond of sympathy between him and the speaker or poet,
who has typically done the same thing"; this is precisely the reading
process evoked, for instance, in *Clarissa* and outlined in detail in

Rambler 60. Indeed, Rothstein concludes his important article with a challenge to criticism which my study, however modestly, is designed to address.

If imaginative expansion, visual and nonvisual, was as widespread and significant as I have alleged, modern critical opinion must accommodate it in dealing with eighteenth-century works, written or painted with formal, affective criteria so sharply different from those of the aesthetic purism now commonly practiced. We must develop critical techniques for it better than the simple applause or frown to which too many practical critics of the eighteenth century resorted when faced with indeterminacy.[8]

In three quite precise ways I will discuss how the expectation of a detached or impossible observer is challenged by the presence of indeterminacy in eighteenth-century prose. First, all the works I examine, which cover a wide generic and authorial range, are structured around one or more spectator characters or authors who wish to observe or report about a situation, but who eventually become a part of the very situation they initially set out to describe. In some cases the loss of detachment is unwitting; in other instances detachment is knowingly and sometimes willingly abandoned. In every case, however, the appearance of detachment is designed to elicit a distinction between the expectation of rational control and the eventual yielding to an experience whose effect supersedes the strict control of reason. The second way that the impossible observer appears is in the author's use of what I call reading paradigms. I am not fond of jargon, but this is the only term that describes exactly what I wish to say. By reading paradigms, I mean particular passages, found in every work I will consider, which are not about the story, the characters, the ideas, or the arguments so much as they are about the reader and how to read the book. In these situations the author, for a variety of reasons, anticipates our (that is, the reader's) customary role of detached observer, and addresses himself to our expectations; this is done to draw us into the book, to make us, willing or not, participants rather than just observers, and to test our strength in relation to the author's assumptions about human nature.[9] Lastly, I will apply the idea of the impossible observer to the way criticism has attempted to deal with the experience of reading the selected texts. That is, I will measure the results of my affective approach against prior criticism so as to determine the usefulness of my approach.

The idea of the impossible observer will, I believe, illumine the distinction between objective critical expectations and the basically affective experience of reading.

I should also say that my affective approach is not designed to supplant, but rather to complement, recent studies of eighteenth-century prose. Some of the most interesting modern criticism of fiction generally, and of the eighteenth-century novel in particular, has focused on various theories, implied or explicit, of literary response. The writings of Wolfgang Iser, for example, offer fascinating insights into the phenomenology of reading, and Iser has stressed the importance of the reader's active participation in, rather than detached observation of, various literary texts.[10] This emphasis on the reader's participatory acts—on the sympathetic appeal of fiction—has also been applied, in a number of ways, in three books devoted exclusively to eighteenth-century prose: John Preston's *The Created Self* (New York: Barnes and Noble, 1970), John A. Dussinger's *The Discourse of the Mind in Eighteenth-Century Fiction* (The Hague: Mouton, 1974), and Eric Rothstein's *Systems of Order and Inquiry in Later Eighteenth-Century Fiction* (Berkeley and Los Angeles: University of California Press, 1975). In each case, though from different methodological points of view, these works have repeatedly stressed the activity of reading and the affective appeal of eighteenth-century fiction. In the latter two books, moreover, Dussinger and Rothstein have attempted, with varying degrees of success, to establish relationships between the affective appeal of eighteenth-century prose and the prevailing epistemological constructs of the century.

I certainly see my own book as participating in, and benefiting from, the arguments of the above books. At the same time, however, I must say that my affective approach takes its primary impetus from the critical works of Samuel Johnson. From Johnson's criticism I have cheerfully drawn the following critical formulations, all of which flow from the basic distinction, established in *The Life of Cowley*, between beholding and partaking of literature. Although I will examine Johnson's criticism in more detail in chapters 6 and 9, I am convinced that he is opposed to the idea of what I call the impossible observer. I believe this is why he prefers Richardson's "characters of nature," whose affective appeal is directly related to the powerful indeterminacy of much of Richardson's fiction, to Fielding's "characters of manners," who conform more readily with a self-contained, highly Aristotelian,

and easily recognizable aesthetic design. Indeed, it is especially revealing to watch how Johnson associates "characters of manners" with
simple entertainment and superficial observation: "Sir, (continued he,)
there is all the difference in the world between characters of nature and
characters of manners; and *there* is the difference between the characters of Fielding and those of Richardson. Characters of manners are
very entertaining; but they are to be understood, by a more superficial
observer, than characters of nature, where a man must dive into the
recesses of the human heart."[11] Although I do not share Johnson's
view that Fielding is superficial, I do think that Johnson is attempting
to describe, however unfairly, two different kinds of narrative: the one
oriented to character and psychology and thus tending toward indeterminacy, the other oriented to plot and overt action and hence much
more determinate. We might also recall, critical opinion notwithstanding, that Johnson claimed he "read Fielding's *Amelia* through without
stopping"—for reasons that should be clear when I discuss *Clarissa*
and *Amelia*.[12]

Moreover, I believe that Johnson is opposed to an excessive preoccupation with genre and with critical taxonomy generally, as we can
see in his Shakespeare criticism, because an obsession with generic
distinctions and rules often blunts the powerful affective appeal of literature. This is why Johnson, in his edition of Shakespeare, so often
attacks Warburton's strictly literary understanding of Shakespeare. Furthermore, I am attracted to Johnson's formulation of a common reader,
though it is an extremely slippery concept: the common reader, as I
understand it, is less a verifiable *who* than an experiential *how*—that is,
not a specific person, but rather a general process of reading literature
which supersedes rational objectivity even as it asserts a cognitive and
moral basis for the affective appeal of literature. This sense of a "uniformity of sentiment" is the basis of Johnson's keen understanding and
vigorous defense of Shakespeare's use of tragicomedy. In my view,
then, Johnson is ultimately less important as a critic of literature—that
is, as one who systematically explicates or theorizes about a literary
work—than as a reader of literature who insistently focuses on its affective appeal, and who repeatedly debunks objective critical expectations.

Finally, the critical model that Johnson employs has led me to
believe that, though the authors I include go about their appeals to
human experience in a variety of ways, there rests beneath this variety
a fundamentally similar challenge. This challenge is addressed to what I

call the impossible observer—to the critical procedure, not to say human expectation, which assumes, consciously or unconsciously, that the exercise of reason is a satisfactory tool for understanding and assessing the appeal of imaginative literature. Both in their represented actions and in their effects on the reader, the works I shall discuss continually evoke and test the reader's awareness of the problematical aspects of human reason, and they often require the reader's abandonment of critical objectivity to the more compelling, though less determinate, claims of human feeling. All the works I shall deal with construct occasions where the reader inevitably becomes a part of the very literary representation he may have expected only to observe. This is done not only to challenge the reader's assumed sense of superiority, which is often based on the self-sufficiency of reason, but to remind him that this life, as Richardson said, is "a State of Probation," where the expectations of readers and characters alike are continually the focus of examination.[13]

2
Swift and the Problematical Nature of Meaning

The main problem I shall discuss in this chapter has been raised most acutely by F. R. Leavis in his essay "The Irony of Swift."[1] Leavis begins by examining the disjunction between Swift's ostensible themes, including the moral content of his writings, and the effects his writings have on readers. This disjunction, if we accept it as such, raises important critical questions not only about the kinds of irony and satire that Swift employs, but about the overall moral purpose of Swift's use of irony and satire. And lest we think these questions are the recent invention of modern criticism, let me quote from one of Pope's letters to Swift which establishes some important distinctions between the different uses of irony and satire. Pope writes to Swift: "I have not the courage however to be such a Satyrist as you, but I would be as much, or more, a Philosopher. You call your satires, Libels; I would rather call my satires, Epistles: They will consist more of morality than wit, and grow graver, which you will call duller."[2]

If I read Pope's observations correctly, he is saying that his practice of satire differs from Swift's both in kind and purpose. Swift's satire is courageous, libelous, and witty, which is to say that it is very aggressive and quite often personal. On the other hand, Pope's satire is philosophical, epistolary, and grave—all of which implies, I think, that its appeal is primarily intellectual. To some extent Pope may be echoing the old distinction between Juvenalian and Horatian satire; or, if we want to adopt Edward Rosenheim's useful distinction, we might say that Swift's satire veers toward the "punitive," Pope's toward the "persuasive."[3] In any event, Leavis, too, is quite aware of such distinctions, but unlike Pope and Rosenheim he extends their essentially *descriptive* distinctions into an *evaluative* model for judging the relation between the moral content and the literary effects of Swift's writings. Thus Leavis writes:

There are writings of Swift where "critical" is the more obvious word (and where "intellectual" may seem correspondingly apt)—notably, the pamphlets or pamphleteering essays in which the irony is instrumental, directed and limited to a given end. The *Argument Against Abolishing Christianity* and the *Modest Proposal*, for instance, are discussible in the terms in which satire is commonly discussed: as the criticism of vice, folly, or other aberration, by some kind of reference to positive standards. But even here, even in the *Argument*, where Swift's ironic intensity undeniably directs itself to the defense of something that he is intensely concerned to defend, the effect is essentially negative. The positive itself appears only negatively—a kind of skeletal presence, rigid enough, but without life or body; a necessary precondition, as it were, of directed negation. The intensity is purely destructive. (pp. 16–17)

I have quoted Leavis in such detail because he has raised the central question of whether Swift's use of irony and satire is "discussible in the terms in which satire is commonly discussed." Clearly, we can discuss Swift's satire, both in his poems and prose, as a criticism of vice and folly, but sometimes we cannot do so "by some kind of reference to positive standards." For example, the history of reader responses to *A Tale of a Tub* and *Gulliver's Travels* suggests that Swift certainly vexed the world, but the vexation may itself have been prompted by Swift's inability or unwillingness to sustain a satisfactory "positive standard."[4]

Thus, comparing Gibbon's irony with Swift's, Leavis argues that the "pattern of Gibbonian prose insinuates a solidarity with the reader," whereas "the implied solidarity in Swift is itself ironical—a means to betrayal." Leavis further observes that Gibbon's irony "habituates and reassures," while Swift's is "essentially a matter of surprise and negation; its function is to defeat habit, to intimidate, and to demoralize" (pp. 17–18). The main example that Leavis uses to support the idea that Swift's irony betrays the reader comes from section 9 of *A Tale of a Tub*, specifically the two famous paragraphs on deception and madness.[5] What Leavis attempts to demonstrate (I think quite persuasively) is that the operative thematic distinction between "curiosity" and "credulity" finally cancels itself out, leaving the reader to his own resources. That is, the reader is initially lured into believing that Swift is

attacking "curiosity" in defense of the "common forms" associated
with the Church of England and, by implication, with "credulity."
This part would accord well with Swift's claim that he wrote the *Tale*
"to expose the Abuses and Corruptions in Learning and Religion" (1:6).
But by the end of the second paragraph, which concludes, "This is
the sublime and refined Point of Felicity, called, the *Possession of
being well-deceived*, The Serene Peaceful State of being a Fool among
Knaves" (1:110), the alternative, or, if you will, the positive standard
of "credulity" has itself been undermined.[6] The reader is thus left in a
state of intellectual disorientation, unless, of course, we delight in being
called "a Fool among Knaves."

Now I will be the first to concede that this is a local instance from
A Tale of a Tub, but I would also argue that it is a characteristic effect
of the work; and, far more decisively, Swift's "Apology" confirms his
awareness that the effect of *A Tale of a Tub* was a good deal more
problematical than he evidently intended. Indeed, the "Apology" suggests that Swift miscalculated in at least two distinct ways: he under-
estimated the effect of his own invention and he overestimated the
sagacity of his readers. Throughout the "Apology," for example, Swift
distinguishes between "Men of Tast" (1:1), otherwise referred to as
"the judicious Reader" (1:3, 8, 10), and the "Reader of Tast and
Candor" (1:6), as opposed to those readers "who have neither Candor
to suppose good Meanings, nor Palate to distinguish true Ones" (1:2)
and "prejudiced or ignorant Readers [who] have drawn by great Force
to hint at ill Meanings" (1:4). But the telling point is that Swift is
unable to control how these various readers respond to *A Tale*, even
though he can declare that the work "celebrates the Church of England"
(1:2). In fact, the "Apology" concludes with Swift's concession that
in future readings "it is not unlikely he [Swift] may have the Pleasure
to find twenty Meanings, which never enter'd into his Imagination"
(1:11).

What Swift fails to acknowledge in the "Apology" is the power of
his satire to evoke a wide range of meanings, even though he mocks the
idea that a text may be interpreted as being "wondrous *Deep*, upon no
wiser Reason than because it is wondrous *Dark*" (1:133). That is, at
the same time that Swift ridicules corrupt readings and interpretations,
especially in the allegory of the coats, he continues to taunt and tanta-
lize his readers into further interpretations, with no end in sight. The

"courteous Reader" is advised "to peruse with a world of Application, again and again, whatever I have written upon this Matter" (1:48), and a passage like this is the rule, not the exception, in *A Tale*. Swift will mock "learned" commentators when he cautions them "to proceed with great Caution upon certain dark points, wherein all who are not *Veré adepti*, may be in danger to form rash and hasty Conclusions" (1:70). But when he later divides readers into three classes—"the *Superficial*, the *Ignorant*, and the *Learned*"—he unwittingly predicts, and I would say provokes, the kinds of interpretation he worries over in the "Apology": "It were much to be wisht, and I do here humbly propose for an Experiment, that every Prince in *Christendom* will take seven of the *deepest Scholars* in his Dominions, and shut them up close for *seven* Years, in *seven* Chambers, with a Command to write *seven* ample Commentaries on this comprehensive Discourse. I shall venture to affirm, that whatever Difference may be found in their several Conjectures, they will be all, without the least Distortion, manifestly deduceable from the Text" (1:117–18).

Although it is clear that Swift was dismayed by the range of reader responses to *A Tale*, there is considerable evidence to suggest that in some of his subsequent satires—specifically, *Gulliver's Travels* and *A Modest Proposal*—he calculated for and counted on such distortion, which is to say he revised his expectations about his readers. While it is hardly fresh news to say that Swift's satire frequently implicates his readers, it is important to talk about how he does so, and about what distinguishes such satires as *The Battle of Books*, *The Argument against Abolishing Christianity*, and *The Drapier's Letters* from *Gulliver's Travels* and *A Modest Proposal*. For example, I will argue that one of the differences between the former and latter satires is that Swift's developing anticipation of reader "distortion" is a measure both of his increasing mistrust of the reader's reason and of his diminished expectation of reform. In the former satires Swift relies on the reader's reason to discern the object of his satire, and thus the theme of the satire, if you will, is correspondingly determinate. Another way of stating this matter is to say that in *The Battle of Books*, *The Argument against Abolishing Christianity*, and *The Drapier's Letters* Swift serves as a middleman who simultaneously defends something of value—be it Sir William Temple, ancient learning, the Test Act, or Ireland—as he castigates whatever threatens that value—William Wotton, modern learning, repeal of the Sacramental Test, or England's oppression of Ireland.

But in *Gulliver's Travels* and *A Modest Proposal* Swift is less a middle-man or intermediary than he is an aggressor and adversary who, more than anything else, attacks his readers because he no longer trusts them.

The difference between these two modes of satire is the difference between the expectation of reform and its corresponding reliance on reason, and the desire to "vex" the reader which signals both the aban-donment of reform as well as Swift's bitter acknowledgment of distor-tion—textual, moral, intellectual—as the "normal" state of affairs. Thus Swift declares in *An Answer to a Paper called a Memorial* (1728):

I have now present before me the Idea of some Persons, (I know not in what Part of the World) who spend every Moment of their Lives, and every Turn of their Thoughts while they are awake, (and probably of their Dreams while they sleep) in the most detestable Actions and Designs; who delight in *Mischief*, *Scandal*, and *Obloquy*, with the *Hatred* and *Contempt* of all Mankind against them; but chiefly of those among their own Party, and their own Family; such, whose *odious Qualities* rival each other for Perfection: *Avarice*, *Brutality*, *Faction*, *Pride*, *Malice*, *Treachery*, *Noise*, *Impudence*, *Dulness*, *Ignorance*, *Vanity*, and *Revenge*, contending every Moment for Superiority in their Breasts. Such Creatures are not to be reformed; neither is it Prudence, or Safety to attempt a Reformation. Yet, although their Memories will *rot*, there may be some benefit for their Survivers, to smell it while it is *rotting*. (12:24–25)

This is the characteristic tone of *Gulliver's Travels* and *A Modest Proposal*, and the underlying reasons for Swift's abandonment of refor-mation and reason are illumined by P. K. Elkin, who observes: "Au-gustan satire was firmly rooted in the comforting conviction of the age that men are free and responsible beings, who can set about improving themselves and their society by the exercise of reason. . . . Such faith in free will and the efficacy of reason made men unusually eager to increase knowledge and to raise themselves and society to a more highly civilized level; and with notable exceptions, like Swift and Mandeville, it made them extraordinarily confident of their ability to achieve such a goal." [7] Elkin is right to mark off Swift (in some of his satires) and Mandeville as exceptions, though Mandeville's satire, as I shall later argue, addresses its readers in a way different from Swift's. But the critical question that Elkin's observation suggests is, How does an attack on "the efficacy of reason" affect and implicate the reader's relation to satire? In other words, how do we talk about satires where the subject is the audience for whom the satire is intended—where the meaning, so to say, is not an object in the text, but the responses evoked by the text?

For example, on the most practical and obvious levels *Gulliver's Travels* and *A Modest Proposal* continually address themselves to the subject of the reader's response.[8] They do so, in large measure, by presenting observer narrators who, though initially confident of the self-sufficiency of reason, willingly or unwillingly become participants, and sometimes victims, of the very actions they wish to describe with rational detachment. On a more complicated level, the affective appeal of *Gulliver's Travels* and *A Modest Proposal* depends heavily on their establishment of a sense of bewilderment or shock which challenges our habitual ways of reading and thinking. Moreover, I believe that *Gulliver's Travels* and *A Modest Proposal*, in the most uncanny way, are written in anticipation of the reader's subsequent needs for, and attempts to discern, meaning. They are works whose largest subject is the problematical nature of meaning. Thus, I do not wish to advance some single interpretation of either of these works so much as to deal with some of the ways that Swift plays with and rearranges the reader's expectations of apprehending some discernible meaning even if it is not, strictly speaking, within the text.

The kinds of meaning I have in mind are highly provisional simply because they tend to be evoked, rather than contained, by the text. These meanings are not like objects waiting to be found in the text; they are a set of experiences, doubtless varying with each reader, which grow out of the interaction between the reader's rational expectations and assumptions and the various "events"—including single words and sentences—which establish the affective appeal of *Gulliver's Travels* and *A Modest Proposal*. When I talk about "meanings," then, in *Gulliver's Travels* and *A Modest Proposal* I am simply trying to call attention to some of the ways in which these two works do not so much construct a stable meaning in the form of clearly stated, coherent, and verifiable truths within a text, as they present contexts or occasions for the reader to supply meanings in response to what occurs within the text. Furthermore, while I accept the usefulness of Rosenheim's formulation that "*satire consists of an attack by means of a manifest fiction upon discernible historic particulars*," I am going to concentrate on how Swift "breaks" his manifest fictions to widen the effects of his satire.[9]

First, let me take up the relationship between the manifest fictions

Swift sets up in books 1 and 2—these fictions being Gulliver's size in relation to the Lilliputians and Brobdingnagians—and the statements in the text which are, presumably, outgrowths of the manifest fictions. I use the term "manifest fiction" simply to contrast the seemingly *palpable* apperance of Swift's literary fictions—so conspicuously fictional as well as so seductively simple—with their frequently complicated effects. Many critics, especially rhetorical and generic critics, have argued for the need to discriminate between Swift and Gulliver and between Swift's fictional forms and what might be called realistic representation.[10] We all know about the quarrels concerning how to construe the Yahoos and Houyhnhnms, but I wish to start with the effects of phrases and sentences in order to show how Swift extends the range of effects by broadening the apparent simplicity of the manifest fictions. Indeed, the simplicity of these fictions is often a parody of rational distinctions, as I shall discuss later. It is my belief that if Swift kept constantly to the maintenance of his manifest fictions, *Gulliver's Travels* would remain primarily self-referring, which is to say the reader would respond to the text as pure fantasy.

For example, a sentence such as the following is completely determined by the big/little fiction of book 1 and hence simply calls attention to its own fiction; about his visit to Mildendo, Gulliver writes: "I stept over the great *Western* Gate, and passed very gently, and sideling through the two principal Streets, only in my short Waistcoat, for fear of damaging the Roofs and Eves of the Houses with the Skirts of my Coat" (11:46). At most, this sentence encourages the reader to imagine a picture of Gulliver's size, wholly consistent with the manifest fiction of book 1, which is both fantastic and humorous. For the reader, entertainment seems to be the principal effect of this passage. A slightly more complicated sentence, in terms of effect, occurs when the Lilliputian soldiers walk across Gulliver's body: "I confess I was often tempted, while they were passing backwards and forwards on my Body, to seize Forty or Fifty of the first that came in my Reach, and dash them against the Ground" (11:24). Such a sentence again preserves the manifest fiction of size but it introduces some recognizably human emotions—emotions the reader has doubtless known. We know what it feels like to be threatened and some, if not all of us, have felt the urge to be violent. Even with these associations, however, this sentence remains basically self-referring inasmuch as the passage, compared with others to be discussed, does not in any serious way address itself to the reader's expectation of and search for meaning.

On the other hand, the well-known sections of book 1 dealing with rope-dancing, the high and low Heels, and the Little-Endians and Big-Endians are of a rather different order than the two sentences hitherto mentioned. It is not so much the relations of size, in accordance with Swift's use of manifest fictions, as the consequence of establishing at once rational and trivial distinctions which appears to be the principal subject of these sections. To put it another way, these passages are constructed in such a way that the reader is encouraged to break the manifest fictions and extend their significance beyond the text. The reader is compelled to translate back and forth between the manifest fictions and his experience of his own world and the world at large. The reader moves, that is, from detached observation to active participation, for the effect of such passages is to widen the text's meaning beyond Gulliver's observations. The following passage on rope-dancing is a good example.

This Diversion is only practised by those Persons, who are Candidates for great Employments, and high Favour, at Court. They are trained in this Art from their Youth, and are not always of noble Birth, or liberal Education. When a great Office is vacant, either by Death or Disgrace, (which often happens) five or six of those Candidates petition the Emperor to entertain his Majesty and the Court with a Dance on the Rope; and whoever jumps the highest without falling, succeeds in the office. (11:38)

We need not tie this activity down either to the fictional world of Lilliput or to specific historical persons, though I am not denying either interpretive possibility. But the opening sentence does permit us to add numerous examples from the past or present to the general category of "Persons, who are Candidates for great Employments, and high Favour, at Court." With the exception of the term "rope-dancing" everything in this passage can refer to the reader's, and not just Gulliver's world, and the sheer familiarity of external references surrounding the manifest fiction of rope-dancing encourages the reader to translate the fictional image into the human arena of political aspirations and ambitions generally. Thus, what initially appears to be a purely fictional description is also the occasion for a much larger, and more problematical, appeal to the reader's awareness.

For example, to the extent that the reader is a person rigidly com-

mitted to the numerous and often trivial abstractions of politics, religion, and class distinctions, Swift's explanation of the high and low
Heels and the Big- and Little-Endians may set off a good deal of uneasiness, simply because what was expected to remain a self-referring
fiction suddenly intrudes upon our personal convictions. Of course, we
can always say that Swift is really referring to Whigs and Tories, High
Church and Low Church, but then Swift early realized that readers have
a habit of beholding "every body's Face but their Own" (1:140). Nevertheless, observations such as "He [the Emperor of Lilliput] is taller by
almost the Breadth of my Nail, than any of his Court; which alone
is enough to strike an Awe into the Beholders" (11:30), or "His Majesty's Imperial Heels are lower at least by a *Drurr* than any of his Court;
(*Drurr* is a Measure about the fourteenth Part of an Inch.)" (11:48)
evoke the reader's awareness not only of the arbitrary niceties that
are the domain of royalty, but of some of the dubious distinctions—
as well as the seemingly rational habits which lead to their creation—
that the reader may unconsciously accept or consciously sustain.[11] If
such a response is provoked, the reader is no longer an observer; like
Gulliver, he becomes a participant, possibly even a victim, of the very
action that he only wished to observe and describe. Indeed, one of the
ironies of critical debates over book 4 of *Gulliver's Travels* is that some
critics have duplicated Swift's fictional premise of Big-Endians and
Little-Endians by aligning themselves into the so-called "hard-school"
and "soft school," or what might be called the "Hard-Endians" and
"Soft-Endians"—all of which is wonderfully reminiscent of Swift's
droll observation that "Satyr being levelled at all, is never resented for
an offence by any, since every individual Person makes bold to understand it of others, and very wisely removes his particular Part of the
Burthen upon the shoulders of the World, which are broad enough, and
able to bear it" (1:31).

So far I have been talking generally about how Swift breaks and
extends the frame of reference of his manifest fictions to establish a
larger, affective appeal to the reader's own experiences. I have tried to
emphasize, albeit briefly, the variety of effects Swift's text produces
simply because such variety seems to me strong evidence that *Gulliver's
Travels* is not written with any one effect in mind, other than to violate
or vex the reader's expectations of coherent, rationally formulable
meaning. Rather than reading *Gulliver's Travels* as if it were proceed-
ing towards some one coherent and unifying goal, it may be truer to the

reader's experience of the text to speak of a succession of moments that yield varying effects. In book 2, for example, the manifest fiction of size can yield a self-referring and humorous sentence such as, "She [the farmer's daughter] was very good natured, and not above forty Foot high, being little for her Age" (11:95), or a more potentially offensive passage which grows out of, but extends beyond, the manifest fiction's ostensible frame of reference—"I must confess no Object ever disgusted me so much as the Sight of her monstrous Breast, which I cannot tell what to compare with, so as to give the curious Reader an Idea of its Bulk, Shape and Colour. It stood Prominent six Foot, and could not be less than sixteen in Circumference. The Nipple was about half the Bigness of my Head, and the Hue both of that and the Dug so varied with Spots, Pimples and Freckles, that nothing could appear more nauseous. . . . This made me reflect upon the fair Skins of our *English* ladies" (11:91–92). Here the transference from manifest fiction to the reader's experience is not simply encouraged; it is, perhaps dismayingly, insisted upon.

One of the most famous sections of book 2—Gulliver's praise of his "own dear native Country" to the king of Brobdingnag—gains much of its effectiveness by continually crossing and finally obscuring the lines between the established manifest fiction of size, Gulliver's descriptions of England, and the reader's uneasy intervention into the process. The reader may not agree either with Gulliver's praise or the king's subsequent condemnation of the bulk of mankind, but the locutions of this sixth chapter of the book—i.e., "Conspiracies, Rebellions, Murders, Massacres, Revolutions, Banishments; the very worst Effects that Avarice, Faction, Hypocrisy, Perfidiousness, Cruelty, Rage, Madness, Hatred, Envy, Lust, Malice and Ambition could produce" (11:132)—are sufficiently familiar to the reader that he cannot fail to recognize an aspect of his own world even if he feels compelled to attach explanations, provisos, and even apologies throughout the entire chapter. Indeed, this very compulsion to explain testifies to the effectiveness of the chapter. The one seemingly fictional assertion referring back to size in the last paragraphs of chapter 6—that "the Bulk of your Natives [are] . . . the most pernicious Race of little odious Vermin that Nature ever suffered to crawl upon the Surface of the Earth"—joins the ostensibly separate levels of fiction and fact in the most paradoxical way. Men are not literally "vermin," but the reader is led to understand, and may even endorse, the literal applicability of this seemingly figurative expression. The king's concluding remarks strike me as a fine example of the multiple collision between the various modes of writing Swift employs, the affective appeal of the text, and the reader's attempt to determine, and possibly deflect, the meaning of the passage. We may wish to introduce affirmative examples to deny Gulliver's descriptions of the king's accusations, we may reject or defend the king's peroration as either unwarranted or justified misanthropy, we may wish to argue for or against the fictional consistency or inconsistency of this chapter as part of a literary satire, and there may be, depending on the reader, numerous additional responses. But one thing is clear: the reader is compelled to react to this section in terms that extend beyond a purely fictional or literary frame of reference; we are no longer observers of a fiction, but participants in it. In this respect Swift has successfully forced us into a form of reexamination where ratiocination alone simply will not do. The meanings of this section, in other words, are not so much within the text as in the reader's response—emotional and intellectual—to the text.

Having established my own position with respect to some of the effects of *Gulliver's Travels*, I would like to direct some attention to two larger questions which have vexed general readers and critics alike. Again, I entertain no hope of solving these "problems," because I believe that *Gulliver's Travels*, among other things, renders highly problematical the reader's expectation of arriving at rational "solutions" to his own uneasiness. The first of these two questions relates to the function of book 3 both in terms of its content and its larger structural position with respect to the other three books; the second, to the matter of how to interpret the Houyhnhnms. My general position, based on the affective appeal of *Gulliver's Travels*, is that we should be neither surprised nor distressed by the varying and sometimes contradictory positions taken with respect to these two problems. They are problems and will remain problems because the determination of meaning in *Gulliver's Travels* is not strictly amenable to rational inspection.

Book 3, we know, was written last, and yet Swift does not place it in this position. The fact that Swift does not place it last may tell us something about his attitude to formal coherence—namely, that there never was a developing pattern or an evolving plan which would explain the sequence of books 1–4, other than the general intention to vex the reader. I have emphasized that Swift will use and perhaps abuse his manifest fictions in a variety of ways to gain multiple effects ranging from comedy to declamation. So I am no longer surprised that book 3 occupies its particular structural position, simply because I do not believe the structure of *Gulliver's Travels* was, in any formal sense, ever determined by building toward any one coherent pattern. In fact, here I would enlarge the significance of what is evident in individual phrases and sentences of books 1 and 2 and argue that we should make a distinction between formal coherence within a text (what might be called embedded meaning) and the reader's rational expectation of detecting such coherence. The former kind of coherence is virtually nonexistent in *Gulliver's Travels*—I say "virtually" because I suppose one could say that books 1 and 2 employ a manifest fiction of comparative size which accounts, in part, for their structural sequence. The latter *expectation* of coherence certainly exists because we as readers are always looking for what a literary text is about and how it makes sense. In this latter respect, however, I would say it is the reader rather than the text who substantially creates the meaning.

Thus, if one looks for a pattern within book 3 it appears that Gulliver for long periods of time—in his attacks on the Academy of Lagado, politicians, and modern history—seems very reliable, in Wayne Booth's sense of the term. Moreover, Gulliver utters sentences and attacks positions and activities which Swift himself has attacked in his nonironic essays and in his correspondence. But just when the reader believes he may have achieved a fixed position on Gulliver's reliability, Swift introduces the Struldbrugg episode which, among other things, mocks Gulliver's expectation of immortality and thus creates for the reader another occasion where detached observation lapses into unwitting participation. The arguments, therefore, over the apparent "disunity" of book 3 are really confirmations of the view that the appeal of *Gulliver's Travels* actually exceeds and eludes the grasp of rational predictability. Once again Swift has used book-reading habits and conventions—that is, the confidence that books evolve coherently toward a determinate conclusion—to violate the reader's expectation of meaning so as to extend the effect of the manifest fiction from a purely literary frame of reference to the more problematical nature of the reader's attempts to discern and sustain meaning.

For me to speak in such lofty philosophical terms as "the problematical nature of meaning" involves the risk of making Swift out to be a philosopher of sorts, and we all know that Swift rarely expressed admiration for the "transcendentals" of philosophy. But the evidence is irrefutable that throughout his career Swift demonstrates an understanding of language—of how it can create and destroy meaning—second to that of few authors in the history of English literature. To think of Swift's writing career is to think of the career of a prose writer who achieved the widest spectrum of literary effects, and that spectrum is contained in miniature in *Gulliver's Travels*. It is precisely because this range of literary effects, as distinguished from the concentrated effect of, say, *An Argument against Abolishing Christianity*, is used in *Gulliver's Travels* that Swift achieves in this work a unique anticipation of the very distortion that so dismayed him in *A Tale of a Tub*. Meaning becomes problematical in *Gulliver's Travels* because Swift chooses to put all his verbal skills on display—his skills for fantasy, humor, mimicry, parody, attack, ridicule, and just convolution for its own sake—and they are not directed toward any one specifiable meaning. This is why, for example, so many different and apparently contradictory critical approaches have been applied to the Houyhnhnms. Strictly speaking, the Houyhnhnms are not in the least problematical: they are a manifest fiction employed by Swift, the nature of their representation being, generally, "the Contemplation and Practice of every Virtue" (11:258). This, at any rate, is their ostensible meaning within the text. But as with so many other manifest fictions in *Gulliver's Travels*, Swift does not keep the Houyhnhnms on a purely self-referential level; they become occasions for a much larger appeal. He breaks the manifest fiction repeatedly—either through Gulliver's extension of their frame of reference or by encouraging or forcing the reader to extend the range of their significance.

Insofar as the following passage refers to the exclusive fictional properties of the Houyhnhnms, it is not problematical; but as soon as any point of human reference emerges, the passage reflects outward to the reader, and may evoke (indeed, has evoked) a variety of responses:

As these noble *Houyhnhnms* are endowed by Nature with a general disposition to all Virtues, and have no Conceptions or Ideas of what is evil in a rational Creature; so their grand Maxim is, to cultivate *Reason*, and to be wholly governed by it. Neither is *Reason* among them a Point problematical as with us, where men can argue with Plausibility on both Sides of a Question; but strikes you with immediate Conviction; as it must needs do where it is not mingled, obscured, or discoloured by Passion and Interest. I remember it was with ex-

treme Difficulty that I could bring my Master to understand the Meaning of the
Word *Opinion*, or how a Point could be disputable; because *Reason* taught us to
affirm or deny only where we are certain; and beyond our Knowledge we cannot
do either. (11:267).

   The first sentence of this passage defines the Houyhnhnms both in
terms of their self-referential fictional quality and in terms of a radical
contrast with their fictional counterparts, the Yahoos, whose disposition
is to nastiness and dirt. But the first quoted sentence does more than
simply define and distinguish virtue and vice, Right Reason and the
defective uses of reason: it engages the reader and his experience by
employing terms that customarily belong to the world at large, the
world of so-called reality. Thus, to the extent that such terms as *reason*
and *evil* are used by us with confidence, the meaning of this first
sentence becomes problematical, both because these familiar terms encourage us to break the fiction and translate back and forth between
our world and the world of the Houyhnhnms and because in extending
the fiction's frame of reference, we become aware of how difficult it is
to arrive at any universally acceptable definition of such terms as reason
and evil, even though we may feel that we know what reason is. The
fact is we do have "Conceptions or Ideas of what is evil," and while
we may share the Houyhnhnms' laudable desire for the cultivation of
reason we may also wonder whether we are or ever have been "wholly
governed by it." In other words, before we know it we are responding
to a manifest fiction because that fiction is implicating us; like Gulliver,
we, too, end up conversing with, or at least about, horses. Once again,
we move from observation to participation, whether we like it or not;
in fact, observation becomes the occasion for participation. Lest we
have any doubts about our being implicated by Swift's fiction, the
second sentence of this passage begins: "Neither is *Reason* among them
a Point problematical as with us." Who is "us?"—certainly not Gulliver and the Houyhnhnms, nor even Gulliver and the Yahoos, but
Gulliver and his readers. Again, the self-referential dimension of the
fiction is broken and explicitly widened. This passage, it turns out, is
about "us"—maybe even more so than about the Houyhnhnms. We are
compelled, possibly even coerced, to answer back, for reason is indeed
a "Point problematical" with "us." We are, after all, literary critics!
And the third sentence taunts our understanding of reason, for we do

traffic in "*Opinions*" and we find it impossible "to affirm or deny only where we are certain." We may find it impossible precisely because it is our opinion that rational certainty is unavailable.

What I am trying to say—what this passage encourages me to say—is that as the text itself denies uncertainty and insists on clarity, mocking perhaps the reader's customary expectation and need for closure and a sense of certitude, I am compelled to qualify, if not reject, its clarity and plead for uncertainty, at least partly to save my own skin. Such a response, strictly speaking, is not empirically verified by the text, for my response does not exist in a one-to-one relation with some sort of meaning within the test. Rather, the text coerces me to respond and forces me to become a participant in its action, a participant who pleads for the limitations of rational observation, even as he laments the loss of "Right Reason." I do feel uneasy with this passage—I *still* do for a variety of "reasons." So I begin to explain and I think Swift expects me to do so. But as I explain, I am really testifying, like it or not, to the affective appeal of *Gulliver's Travels*, for it has evoked from me the consciousness of the problematical nature of reason as a tool for determining and asserting meaning.

To this point I have not tried to specify a single all-inclusive definition of satire in *Gulliver's Travels*, mainly because I wish to resist the tendency of critics to have some formula in mind before they set out to discuss this work. In emphasizing the variety of its effects (maybe satire *is* a "mixed dish"), I have tried to loosen up this formulaic impulse. However, I believe that *Gulliver's Travels*, insofar as it raises in the reader's mind the consciousness of the problematical nature of meaning, violates our formulaic procedures in order to expand the reader's awareness of his own personal needs, public commitments, and intellectual habits and expectations. Swift does not simply tell us to rethink or reexamine this and that position or assumption; rather he continually creates occasions in the text which change the reader from an observer to a participant by leading him to an awareness of the limitations of reason. The use of reason, for example, is not simply a topic in *Gulliver's Travels* (i.e., "I have got materials Towards a Treatis proving the Falsity of that Definition *animal rationale;* and to show it should be only rationis capax").[12] Rather it is the principal occasion for Swift's compelling challenge to one of the fundamental bases of the reader's life. We are never permitted for long to remain detached, because this

would presume the superiority of the reader's reason; instead we are
sucked into the maelstrom of Swift's epistemological challenges and
hence we frequently feel disoriented and uneasy. In fact, maybe this is
what Swift had in mind when he wrote Pope, "I tell you after all that I
do not hate Mankind, it is vous autres who hate them because you
would have them reasonable Animals and are Angry for being dis-
appointed" (*Correspondence*, 3:118). One implication of this quotation is that *Gulliver's Travels* is designed to elicit the reader's sense of
disappointment when he cannot rationally explain, nor remain detached
from, the cumulative effect of Swift's satire.

Here I am tempted to mention, very tentatively, a procedure (not a
definition) that may be operating in some of Swift's satires. The procedure is this: that in many of these works Swift tends to employ manifest
fictions as a device for exposing, analyzing, and often undercutting the
latent fictions—such as the uninspected reliance on reason—of ordinary
human life. I would take this description one step further and remark
that many of Swift's satires begin with a manifest fiction—be it a proposal or the creation of a fictional world—that initially seems totally
foreign to the reader's ordinary life (a sort of external embodiment of
detached observation), but as the satire proceeds Swift continually de-
creases the distance between the manifest fiction and the reader's world
in order to draw the reader into participating in what he only expected
to observe.

Let me try to make this description more concrete by looking briefly
at a more concentrated work, *A Modest Proposal*, which is narrated by
another observer figure. There are at least two movements in this work
whose rationale Swift has well described in *A Short View of the State
of Ireland*: "There is not one Argument used to prove the Riches of
Ireland, which is not a logical demonstration of its Poverty" (12:11).
In other words, the same method of reasoning, with respect to the state
of Ireland, can be used to produce contradictory conclusions. But it is
not so much the contradictory conclusions which matter; it is that these
conclusions are the result of a process—the law of the excluded middle,
for example—which the reader expects to lead to one consistent meaning rather than several contradictory meanings. Moreover, the text of
A Modest Proposal does not simply tell us that this is so; the experience
of reading the text yields these contradictory conclusions, and in doing
so elicits from the reader some peculiar effects.

Roughly the first quarter of *A Modest Proposal* deals with the ostensible subject of "*the present deplorable State of the Kingdom*" (12: 109). The speaker logically demonstrates the poverty of Ireland, and from this logical demonstration he draws a conclusion sufficiently shocking that the reader, or at any rate most readers, will respond to his proposal of cannibalism as a palpable fiction designed for shock purposes. A certain amount of uneasiness sets in at this point—first because the proposal itself is shocking and secondly because it has been arrived at through the apparently bona fide processes of reasoning. At this point the reader is perhaps left muttering, "This proposal can't be serious," because though the proposal is demonstrably rational, it is also morally appalling. Roughly the last three-fourths of *A Modest Proposal* logically demonstrates, among other things, that the very poverty of Ireland may be used as a source for, and proof of, its riches. The fact of starvation is here shown to be a potential source of food, clothing, and revenue. Once again, it is not just the conclusion drawn by the speaker which matters, but the manner in which he arrives at his conclusion. He has employed the kinds of processes we associate with reasoning, but because we may find his proposal morally appalling, we are left in a state of mind psychologists call "approach-avoidance." We are at once attracted to the method—to the extent, at any rate, that we regard ourselves as logical, reasoning people who think, moreover, that conditions of poverty ought to be ameliorated—but we are repelled by the conclusion because cannibalism, at least in Western society, is wholly rejected.

But Swift does not stop here, for there still exists some distance between the reader and the speaker's proposal. Instead, as in so many places in *Gulliver's Travels*, Swift breaks the apparently fictional proposal of cannibalism and insinuates, if not insists on, its virtual authenticity. The italicized section beginning after the statement "Therefore, let no man talk to me of other Expedients" (12:116) in fact enumerates, as other commentators have noticed, the many and diverse proposals Swift made in his own person concerning the deplorable state of Ireland. Just a cursory look, for example, at *A Proposal for the Universal Use of Irish Manufacture*, or *A Short View of the State of Ireland*, or *An Answer to a Paper Called a Memorial* will demonstrate the irrefutable correlation between the italicized section and Swift's, as opposed to his speaker's, real convictions. But the far more important matter concerns why Swift chooses to break his fiction and call attention to his own biographical presence. One possible answer, which bears directly on my description of Swift's procedures, is that he wishes to decrease and eventually obscure the distinction between the speaker's modest proposal and Swift's own prior proposals in order to emphasize that there is a real (as opposed to fictional) sense in which the proposal approaches historical certitude. It is not that Swift wants cannibalism or believes in cannibalism, but rather that given the actual historical facts —including the present state of Ireland and Swift's prior proposals for improving the state of Ireland—there is sufficient plausibility in the speaker's proposal of cannibalism because it is almost the only method of "improvement" left to be tried.

The italicized section, in other words, momentarily collapses our customary distinctions between satire and straightforward belief in order to demonstrate that all other avenues of improving Ireland's deplorable state have been exhausted. Out of this awareness emerges the problematical and necessarily disorienting effect of *A Modest Proposal:* namely, that what initially appeared to be a grotesque but palpable fiction, advanced by an ostensibly fictional speaker, may also be construed as a reasonably accurate historical estimate of, and solution to, the deplorable state of Ireland. The manifest fiction has approached fact and the reader necessarily squirms with uneasiness. For precisely at the point where the observer narrator declares his rational impartiality, his detachment dramatizes the moral insufficiency of the use of reason he so confidently defends: "I profess, in the Sincerity of my Heart, that I have not the least personal Interest, in endeavouring to promote this necessary Work; having no other Motive than the *publick Good of my Country, by advancing our Trade, providing for Infants, relieving the Poor, and giving some Pleasure to the Rich*" (12:118). The effect of this passage is to discredit pure reason as a grotesque fiction by appealing to the very "personal Interest" the narrator disclaims. The use of reason and the experience of reading here collide with one another. That is, *A Modest Proposal* satisfies all the conditions of reasoning, but the effect of the work is to make the reader dissatisfied with such dispassionate reasoning. Like the narrator, the reader may wish and expect to remain a detached observer, but the conditions of such observation would require a grotesque sacrifice of "personal Interest."

Thus the affective appeal of *A Modest Proposal*, like that of *Gulli-*

ver's Travels, derives from Swift's ability to enlarge the reader's awareness by creating a variety of occasions where the reader is led to expect one kind of meaning which is presumed both to exist within the text and to be essentially separable from the reader's life, only to have this expectation violated by Swift's persistent attempts to move back and forth from a seemingly closed system of coherent fictional references to the open and problematical world of the reader's experiences and expectations.

3
Mandeville and the Force of Prejudice

The experience of reading Swift's satire suggests two things: that the principal effect of satire is some experience of disorientation, and that the attempt to define satire reconfirms the original effect of disorientation. The paradox of satire, as both *Gulliver's Travels* and *A Modest Proposal* imply, may well be that at its best it evokes a broad range of effects by moving the reader from a position of rational observation to a discomfiting experience of active participation. To put it another way, satire often generates its meaning by dramatizing the disappointment—to use Swift's word —of the reader's expectation of rationality. At one point in *Free Thoughts on Religion* Mandeville writes, "Few People are acquainted with the force of Prejudice: They are not capable of examining any thing which is rooted into them by Education and Custom." [1] This statement summarizes both the great challenge posed by Mandeville's works and the primary intention from which his works derive their perplexing effects. Mandeville directly confronts his readers with the force of their prejudices, particularly their uninspected assumptions about reason, and he does so by scrupulously examining the foundations of education and custom. To understand and appreciate the perplexing effects of Mandeville's vision requires, therefore, the reader's frequent revision or abandonment of prejudices and preconceptions, including our assumption of formal or aesthetic coherence of literary texts. For Mandeville explicitly acknowledges that *The Fable of the Bees* is "a Rhapsody void of Order or Method." [2]

Between the appearance in 1705 of "The Grumbling Hive" and its reappearance in 1714 as part of *The Fable of the Bees*, Mandeville obviously decided to establish a more intimate contact with the reader's experience. He later specifically attributed (1:

409) the *Fable*'s notoriety to his inclusion in 1723 of "An Essay on Charity and Charity-Schools." No matter how controversial and intimidating the poem *qua* poem may have been, it clearly took on new and wider dimensions when it appeared in 1714 as only a part of—and possibly just the occasion for—a more detailed prose commentary.[3] Mandeville could rail all he wanted about a "*vain*/EUTOPIA *seated in the Brain*" (1:36), but this was familiar and expected stuff coming from a poetic beast fable. Even the octosyllabic couplets—with their rich tradition already exploited by, among others, Rochester and Butler, and subsequently the source of so many of Swift's later satiric poems— no longer had the capacity really to shock a reader, unless, like Swift, the poet employed obscenity to overcome the equilibrium of octosyllabic satires. But Mandeville, to judge by his procedures in "The Grumbling Hive," appears uninterested in obscenity, or unwilling to use it. The content of his poem may be controversial, but the method, in light of Restoration poetic tradition, is predictable and the result is all too familiar. Thus not one of the couplets, not one verse paragraph, in "The Grumbling Hive" has the explosive appeal of the opening sentence of the prose preface to the poem which was added in 1714:

Laws and Government are to the Political Bodies of Civil Societies, what the Vital Spirits and Life itself are to the Natural Bodies of Animated Creatures; and as those that study the Anatomy of Dead carcases may see, that the chief Organs and nicest Springs more immediately required to continue the Motion of our Machine, are not hard Bones, strong Muscles and Nerves, nor the smooth white Skin that so beautifully covers them, but small trifling Films and little Pipes that are either overlook'd, or else seem inconsiderable to Vulgar eyes; so they that examine into the Nature of Man, abstract from Art and Education, may observe, that what renders him a Sociable Animal, consists not in his desire of Company, Good-nature, Pity, Affability, and other Graces of a fair Outside; but that his vilest and most hateful Qualities are the most necessary Accomplishments to fit him for the largest, and according to the World, the happiest and most flourishing Societies. (1:3–4)

Unlike a grumbling hive, with its busy bees performing functions analogous to those of human beings within the poetic structure of a beast fable, this sentence, which is also based on analogy, both seizes the reader's attention and, very likely, assaults his expectations. Hobbes may have generally spoken this way in *Leviathan*, but Mandeville is the master of particulars and, appropriately, of clinical details. In this

sentence Mandeville achieves a stunning effect by inserting such explosive content within the apparent equilibrium of so well-ordered a structure.[4] The sentence, syntactically, is indeed a tour de force, but its
content, I would argue, is designed to demolish the syntactic beauty.
There are "Political Bodies" and "Natural Bodies," a verbal distinction which by the end of the sentence will be collapsed, but Mandeville's principal interest is in how both these bodies function, analogously, as "Machines," and how, to take the analogy further, the
"Machines" are put into motion.

One might wish to argue at this point that Mandeville's use of
analogy performs a function similar to, say, Swift's manifest fictions,
but I think such an argument is fraught with inconsistencies.[5] It is true
that Swift, like Mandeville, is fond of anatomizing mankind, either to
shock or to amuse the reader. But Mandeville's sentence goes beyond
mere shock to the introduction of a basically unfamiliar, or at any rate
unwelcome, system of knowledge which he chooses not to mention and
drop, but to examine, develop, and apply in a basically empirical
manner. As Robert Adolph has noticed, "Mandeville has the sociolo-
gist's instinct to reveal 'what really goes on' under the surface rather
than the outrage emanating from a moral center which characterizes
most satire."[6] The focus, in short, is on the prejudices about reason
the reader has acquired through education and custom, especially the
prejudice that reason and morality go hand in hand. With Mandeville's
Fable, therefore, we need to establish a basic distinction between a
manifest fiction as it appears in Swift's satire, and a latent fiction (or
"prejudice") as it appears in the *Fable*. I do not use this distinction as
a comparison of kinds, but as a way of differentiating between Swift's
use of literary satire and Mandeville's far more empirical approach to
his subject and his readers.

A manifest fiction is a palpably fictional construction—call it Lilliput, Brobdingnag, or rope-dancing—that is used as the occasion for sig-
nifying content, public or personal, which the reader has access to or
is already aware of. A manifest fiction does not have a known meaning
in and of itself; it has meaning only to the extent that it points to something else.[7] A latent fiction, as I use the term, is *not a literary construction*, although it may be the subject of literature; rather it is a tacit
human assumption whose existence is so unquestioned that it has taken
on the status of a truth, or at least appears to be "common sense." Thus

Robert Hopkins, for example, has argued that "Mandeville's use of paradox is intended to highlight in public consciousness the *unstated ambiguities* of the compromises in a possessive individualistic society." [8] When a latent fiction is examined it is inspected for its own sake, not for what it signifies or symbolizes about something else. Unlike a manifest fiction, a latent fiction has a primary meaning of its own; it is not a secondary vehicle or literary construct for some other primary meaning. The disorientation, shock, or disturbance that occurs when a latent fiction is examined—and this does not hold just for satire— derives from the experience that what the reader, and sometimes the author, assumed to be a truth is made problematical. [9] We are shown and made to experience that the primary meaning of a latent fiction is either more or less than what we assumed it to be. Thus the examination of a latent fiction has the capacity to generate new knowledge—for example, M. R. Jack has suggested that Mandeville "anticipates the modern school of behaviorist psychology" [10]—because such an examination consistently employs methods of verification, claiming to describe the reader's world. Moreover, since a latent fiction claims the status of fact, it is often challenged with facts. [11]

If we go back to the one-sentence paragraph already quoted, we can see the difference, albeit in miniature, between a manifest fiction and a latent fiction. Under certain circumstances the asserted analogies between "Political Bodies" and "Natural Bodies," and between the "Anatomy" of physical and political "Carcases" and the concomitant idea that political and natural bodies both are organized like machines by principles of motion, all contain the potential of being metaphors and hence manifest fictions. But Mandeville shortcircuits this fictional usage by insisting on a radical principle of exclusion: first, when he says that he will examine "The Nature of Man, *abstract* [my italics] from Art and Education," and second, when he declares that "*when I say Men, I mean Neither* Jews *nor* Christians; *but meer Man, in the State of Nature and Ignorance of the true Deity*" (1:40). Although it may be tempting to view Mandeville's use of "man in nature" as a manifest fiction, I share Robert Hopkins's view that Mandeville's "'State of Nature' represents an image of early eighteenth-century London society as it really was." Moreover, Mandeville's principle of exclusion enables him to concentrate, as M. R. Jack has argued, on "considering in detail the behavior of fallen man." [12] Such an exclusive

examination of human behavior deprives the reader of the essential
sources of fictional equilibrium. Take away art, education, and religion,
as Mandeville has clearly done, and man, "meer Man," has been
quickly demythologized and is on the verge of being debunked. The
possibility of sustaining manifest fictions, which derive from fictional
procedures, has been effectively removed by Mandeville, chiefly because art, education, and religion are the sources of the very "prejudices" he calls into question.

From my point of view, this paragraph, despite the potential fictional properties of its analogies, is presented as a straightforward analysis
designed to assault the reader's rational expectations. The paragraph is
not, in the mode of *Gulliver's Travels*, intended as literary satire,
though it frequently has the *effect* of satire. It is not satire because it
does not employ manifest fictions; nor is it failed satire, like Defoe's
Shortest Way with Dissenters, because Mandeville at every step is conscious that he is examining latent fictions and challenging their status
as facts with some facts of his own. What Mandeville is also aware of,
however, is that his examination of latent fictions can have an effect
similar to satire because his examination employs many of the stylistic
procedures associated with satire. The juxtaposition, for example, of
"hard Bones, strong Muscles and Nerves," "smooth white Skin,"
over against "small trifling Films and little Pipes," has both the appearance and the effect of a satiric distinction, only Mandeville is capital-
izing on such a distinction not to point to something else beyond the
distinction (i.e., that all that glisters is not gold), but to increase our
consciousness of (and tolerance for) the arbitrary but necessary basis
of the distinction itself. Being the nominalist that he is, Mandeville,
like a satirist, deflates noble generalities with mundane particulars, but
the generalities he deflates—"good Nature, Pity, Affability"—he does
not always wish to destroy. He simply wants to heighten our consciousness of their latent fictional properties, at the same time that he is
willing to concede their necessity as fictions that confer meaning on a
well-ordered, flourishing society.

One could say, perhaps, that Mandeville is a nonfiction satirist.[13]
That is, he uses verifiable details, rather than manifest fictions, to examine the latent fictions of society. But Mandeville rarely attacks or ridicules the need for latent fictions, so long as they are acknowledged as
fictions; indeed, he defends their necessity and usefulness. What he

does attack and ridicule is the belief or expectation that latent fictions are natural, unchanging facts. Even so, Mandeville, unlike Swift, does not attack man's pretension to reason; rather, he assumes that capacity to reason and chooses to widen the reader's understanding of reason. Mandeville continually raises the expectation and promotes the notion that the *Fable of the Bees* will proceed as a wholly rational inquiry devoid of manifest fictions because he expects his reader to be rational. What produces the disorientation—the ostensibly satirical effect—of the inquiry is that, having excluded art, education, and religion, on which so many latent human assumptions rest, he can take familiar concepts thought to be stable, unassailable truths and redefine them in an apparently reasonable manner. Mandeville uses reason to redefine reason and the traditional distinctions that are its products, but he does this not just to ridicule reason, but to give it empirical precision and to provide the reader with a verifiable mode of self-examination, even if such self-examination clashes with one's prejudices.

Mandeville's use of reason is to the traditional uses of reason in his time what logical positivism is to traditional metaphysics: a conceptual reorientation so sweeping in magnitude that it runs the risk, knowingly, of disorientation because it challenges what were taken to be established truths. Like a modern positivist attacking traditional metaphysics, Mandeville writes: *"One of the great Reasons why so few People understand themselves, is that most Writers are always teaching Men what they should be, and hardly ever trouble their heads with telling them what they really are"* (1:39). A sentence like this has the potential of appearing to be a satiric distinction, a distinction designed to humiliate the reader. Traditional satires, after all, do frequently measure events against an assumed standard of "ought." But Mandeville will have none of this: "ought" in the *Fable of the Bees* takes on the status of a manifest fiction. It is purely a device, not a natural fact, and its claim as a natural fact is automatically dismissed. Mandeville's world is the world of "is," where the ethical oughts of art, education, and religion are replaced by the arbitrary "is" of political necessity.

In "An Enquiry into the Origin of Moral Virtue," for example, the idea of civilization, which is so often associated with art, education, and religion, and which is thought to be a well-established and affirmative fact of nature, is shown to be the product of human action and subsequently human design.[14] Instead of considering civilization as a

fact rooted in nature, Mandeville treats its creation as a logical consequence of man's rational awareness of his individual deficiencies. Men
had to be taught to be civilized in order to channel their basically
destructive instincts into the domain of established public order. Man
was not born rational, as so many people thought; he was taught to be
rational for the good of society:

> Those that have undertaken to civilize Mankind, were not ignorant of this;
> but being unable to give so many real Rewards as would satisfy all Persons
> for every individual Action, they were forc'd to contrive an imaginary one.
> . . . They thoroughly examin'd all the Strengths and Frailties of our Nature,
> and observing that none were either so savage as not to be charm'd with Praise,
> or so despicable as patiently to bear Contempt, justly concluded, that Flattery
> must be the most powerful Argument that cou'd be used to Human Creatures.
> (1:42–43)

The chief creations of this process of flattery were "the fine Notions
[Men] had receiv'd concerning the Dignity of Rational Creatures"
(1:45). Reason was made the principal latent fiction on which civilization and social order were based. From the manipulation of reason "the
first Rudiments of Morality, broach'd by skilful Politicians, to render
Men useful to each other as well as tractable, were chiefly contriv'd
that the Ambitious might reap the more Benefit from, and govern vast
Numbers of them with the greater Ease and Security. This Foundation
of Politicks being once laid, it is impossible that Man should long
remain unciviliz'd" (1:47).

The temptation is strong, even in our day, to react to Mandeville's
argument as literary satire. This is because many of us still hold to the
assumption that reason is a fact, not a fiction. But Mandeville's argument is no more satirical, in my view, than B. F. Skinner's arguments
in *Beyond Freedom and Dignity*, where, from the point of view of a
behavioral psychologist, he attempts to demonstrate that freedom, dignity, and the notion of an autonomous reasoning man, are simply words
representing latent fictions that are no longer socially viable because
they cannot account for, and frequently distort, observable facts.

> The picture which emerges from a scientific analysis is not of a body with a
> person inside, but of a body which *is* a person in the sense that it displays a
> complex repertoire of behavior. The picture is, of course, unfamiliar. The man

thus portrayed is a stranger, and from the traditional point of view he may not seem to be a man at all. . . . What is being abolished is autonomous man—the inner man, the homunculus, the possessing demon, the man defended by the literatures of freedom and dignity.

His abolition has long been overdue. Autonomous man is a device used to explain what we cannot explain in any other way. He has been constructed from our ignorance, and as our understanding increases, the very stuff of which he is composed vanishes. Science does not dehumanize man, it de-homunculizes him, and it must do so if it is to prevent the abolition of the human species. To man *qua* man we readily say good riddance. Only by dispossessing him can we turn to the real causes of human behavior. Only then can we turn from the inferred to the observed, from the miraculous to the natural, from the inaccessible to the manipulable. (pp. 190–91)

Very much like Skinner's arguments, Mandeville's examination has the effect of satire because it shakes the equilibrium of familiar concepts which have gained the status of facts. Like Skinner, Mandeville de-homunculizes and ridicules traditional views of man, and his arguments proceed in the same manner as Skinner's. Mandeville, too, turns from the inferred to the observed, from the miraculous to the natural, from the inaccessible to the manipulable. The effect of both books is one of uneasiness and disorientation, for both books demand a radical conceptual reorientation and invite the reader's participation in an unfamiliar, and perhaps unwelcome, form of inquiry. To hear someone speak of civilization as a technology of behavior, to watch someone reduce the concept of reason to the status of a latent fiction, is to feel the *effect* of satire, because so many readers wish to sustain their own form of rational observation.

This effect of satire arises, both in Mandeville and Skinner, from their uncanny and unsettling ability to make the reader self-conscious by associating reason, thought to be a natural good, with the conscious manipulation of human behavior. Mandeville's vocabulary of consciousness, just in the recent passages I have cited, is relentless: "undertaken," "give," "contrive," "examin'd," "observing," "concluded," "used," "broach'd," "render," "reap," "govern," "laid." This is consciousness with a vengeance, so much so that the use of reason takes on the air of a conspiracy to defraud man of his dignity. What is just as annoying and disorienting is that Mandeville has not only used the tool of reason to illumine its status as a latent fiction, but he has used it so effectively that his account of reason, whatever our biases may be, is, at the very least, plausible. Like a persuasive hypothesis, his examination can account for a large number of phenomena; his account is probable because it has predictive capacity, in the sense that it can be used not only to examine but to anticipate human conduct. That is, Mandeville's frequent anticipation of the reader's response is designed to confirm the applicability of his hypothesis.

It is a requirement of reasoning, for example, that one must define terms. This Mandeville does—given his hypothesis about the origin of moral virtue—in an altogether plausible and consistent manner, but not, perhaps, in a welcome and familiar way. Let me cite several definitions spread over the length of *The Fable of the Bees:*

To call every thing, which, without Regard to the Publick, Man should commit to gratify any of his Appetites, VICE; if in that Action there could be observed the least prospect, that it might either be injurious to any of the Society, or render him less serviceable to others. . . . to give the Name of VIRTUE to every Performance, by which Man, contrary to the Impulse of Nature, should endeavour the Benefit of others, or the Conquest of his own Passions out of a Rational Ambition of being good. (1:48–49)

To define then the Reward of Glory in the amplest manner, the most that can be said of it, is, that it consists in a superlative Felicity which a Man, who is conscious of having perform'd a noble Action, enjoys in Self-love, whilst he is thinking on the Applause he expects of others. (1:55)

Pride is that Natural Faculty by which every Mortal that has any Understanding over-values, and imagines better Things of himself than any impartial Judge, thoroughly acquainted with all his Qualities and Circumstances, could allow him. We are possess'd of no other Quality so beneficial to Society, and so necessary to render it wealthy and flourishing as this, yet it is that which is most generally detested. (1:124)

Honour in its Figurative Sense is a Chimera without Truth or Being, an Invention of Moralists and Politicians, and signifies a certain Principle of Virtue not related to Religion, found in some Men that keeps 'em close to their Duty and Engagements whatever they be; as for Example, a Man of Honour enters into a Conspiracy with others to murder a King; he is obliged to go thorough Stitch with it; and if overcome by Remorse or Good nature he startles at the Enormity of his Purpose, discovers the Plot, and turns a Witness against his Accomplices, he then forfeits his Honour, at least among the Party he belong'd to. (1:198–99)

Charity is that Virtue by which part of that sincere Love we have for ourselves is transferr'd pure and unmix'd to others, not tyed to us by the Bonds of Friendship or Consanguinity, and even meer Strangers, whom we have no obligation to, nor hope or expect any thing from. (1:253)

All these definitions conform with Mandeville's empirical and rational principle that "it is impossible to judge of a Man's Performance, unless we are thoroughly acquainted with the Principle and Motive from which he acts" (1:56). Reason, in other words, presumes both consciousness and choice; to deny this, according to Mandeville, is to be irrational. Unlike Swift's many definitions in *Gulliver's Travels*, which grow out of the construction of manifest fictions—the effectiveness of the term "Yahoo," for example, depends considerably on the definition of its fictional counterpart "Houyhnhnm"—Mandeville's definitions are not fictional vehicles referring to something external to the fiction. Mandeville's definitions, while they are shown to be latent fictions that are the products of a latent fiction "reason," are at the same time defended as necessary public facts, as opposed to natural facts. These latent fictions, in and of themselves, have meaning, but it is arbitrarily assigned meaning, in keeping with Mandeville's consistent nominalism. What makes the definitions disorienting is that what were assumed to be natural facts—vice, virtue, pride, honor, charity—are asserted to be the consequence of rational acts and thus subject to human manipulation. What makes these definitions have the effect of satire is that Mandeville backs his reader into a logical dilemma: namely, that if reason presumes consciousness and choice, then all rational definitions must themselves be accessible to consciousness and choice in order to be rational. If, in short, definitions do not yield themselves to empirical demonstration and verification, then such definitions, by the laws of reason, are irrational or at least nonrational.

We can see, again, why Mandeville is so insistent about excluding art, education, and religion from his inquiry; for these forms of knowledge traditionally have been the source of nonrational systems and objects of value (i.e., myth, folklore, mysticism, metaphysics, allegory, faith, etc.). Mandeville's subject is men in nature, which is to say men's actions only as they are accessible to the light of consciousness and demonstration.[15] This is why, for example, Mandeville writes in "Remark (O)": "Thus I have prov'd, that the Real Pleasures of all Men in Nature are worldly and sensual, if we judge from their Practice; I say all Men *in Nature*, because Devout Christians, who alone are to be excepted here, being regenerated, and preternaturally assisted by the Divine Grace, cannot be said to be in nature" (1:166). The key terms of exclusion are "regenerated" and "preternaturally assisted," for they are terms whose referents are not subject to rational demonstration and examination. Mandeville has refined "Devout Christians" out of sight and mind, and such exclusion has the appearance of satire. Similarly, the term "Men *in Nature*" appears to have a satiric effect, but Mandeville's definitions are absolutely consistent and reasonable, in light of his initial premise that reason presumes consciousness and choice.

Because Mandeville excludes all forms of nonrational or suprarational systems of knowledge, he must define all terms in such a way that they conform with man's actions in the public world as distinguished from his intellectual expectations. Mandeville reasons, because he believes it to be in accordance with reason, from practice to principle; or in existential terms, he argues that existence precedes essence. Value is thus not intrinsic. It is created: it is named and defined, not found and described. Accordingly, Mandeville's definitions have the appearance of being "unnatural," which they are, in that they exclude men from allegedly natural sources of value. His definitions are "unnatural" in at least two respects: first, because they are unfamiliar in the sense that they defy common expectations, and secondly because they are fictional creations of man, rather than innate human attributes. Like all definitions, Mandeville's arrest motion for purposes of inspection; but they also cause commotion because they violate, in content, the reader's conventional expectations. Vice and Virtue are no longer viewed as natural qualities; they are qualities imposed by the state to maintain social order. Virtue, thought to be a natural quality by some moralists, is defined as a social good, a proposition with which most of us can cheerfully agree, but Mandeville goes one step further and reminds us that virtue, though a social good, is "contrary to the Impulse of Nature." Mandeville's definition of pride, on the other hand, appears in the first sentence to preserve its traditional aura of disapproval (i.e., *hybris,* the pride before the fall), but again he goes one consistent step further, a step in defiance of traditional ethics, and argues that "no other Quality [is] so beneficial to Society, and so necessary to render it wealthy and flourishing."

What gives so much of *The Fable of the Bees* the appearance and effect of satire is that, like satire, it plays the visible against the latent, the outside against the inside, the action against the motive. However, instead of pushing the reader, as conventional satires do, into the position of either/or, Mandeville demands our tolerant understanding of *both* the inside and outside, the cause and effect, the motive and the action. For example, he at once appeals to our understanding of hypocrisy (a vice in conventional satire) and defends the need for it, as Swift does in *A Project for the Advancement of Religion and the Reformation of Manners* (1709), on the grounds that it preserves social harmony:

It is impossible we could be sociable Creatures without Hypocrisy. The proof of this is plain, since we cannot prevent the Ideas that are continually arising within us, all Civil Commerce would be lost, if by Art and Prudent Dissimulation we had not learn'd to hide and stifle them; and if all we think was to be laid open to others in the same manner as it is to our selves, it is impossible that endued with Speech we could be sufferable to one another. I am persuaded that every Reader feels the Truth of what I say; and I tell my Antagonist that his Conscience flies in his Face, whilst his Tongue is preparing to refute me. (1:349)

Mandeville anticipates, rightly, a negative reaction to his observations on the need for hypocrisy, just as there has been controversy about whether Swift's *Project* is ironic or straightforward.[16] What is perhaps not so well recognized is that any attempt to categorize the above paragraph as palpable satire is itself a form of mistaken refutation, as well as an implied demonstration of the reader's unwillingness to participate in the truth of Mandeville's assertion. To call this satire when Mandeville clearly expects "that every Reader feels the truth of what I say" is to suppress the discomfort of a demonstrable truth in order to defend oneself against a persuasive, but threatening, observation. If the reader refuses to participate in the truth of Mandeville's observation, then he unwittingly confirms the additional truth of Mandeville's remark that "the nearer the Object is the more we suffer" (1:256).

The "Essay on Charity and Charity-Schools" seems not so notorious for its examination of the motives behind charity as for its examination of the social consequences of creating charity schools. Any reader who has read this far through *The Fable of the Bees* would expect

Mandeville to define charity in an entirely rigorous manner and would expect him, if he got around to it, to examine in great detail Dr. John Radcliffe's motives for leaving his fortune to Oxford University. It comes as no surprise, then, that Dr. Radcliffe's motives are examined in light of Mandeville's observation that "Pride and Vanity have built more Hospitals than all the Virtues together" (1:261). This is just another example, by now familiar, of how a private vice may become a public benefit. What is surprising—and judging from the reactions of some of Mandeville's contemporaries downright shocking—is his attack on charity schools, for this attack, among other things, reverses Mandeville's customary habit of defending a private vice as a public benefit. Charity schools have the appearance of being a public benefit, and Mandeville had earlier examined how the impulse behind charity is fundamentally an expression of the vain desire to achieve immortality; but in the case of charity schools Mandeville clearly reverses himself, arguing that this allegedly public benefit, which derives from a private vice, is in fact a public vice because it threatens social order.

Mandeville's argument develops from the premise that "Craft has a greater Hand in making Rogues than Stupidity, and Vice in general is no where more predominant than where Arts and Sciences flourish. Ignorance is, to a Proverb, counted to be the Mother of Devotion, and it is certain that we shall find Innocence and Honesty no where more general than among the most illiterate, the poor silly Country People" (1:269). Lest we be tempted to regard Mandeville's premise as being exclusively satirical—something which evidently many of his contemporaries were *not* tempted to think—let me say straightaway that I believe his argument against charity schools to be no more satirical than Pope's lines in *An Essay on Man*:

> ORDER is Heav'n's first law; and this confest,
> Some are, and must be greater than the rest,
> More rich, more wise; but who infers from hence
> That such are happier, shocks all common sense.
> Heav'n to Mankind impartial we confess,
> If all are equal in their Happiness:
> But mutual wants this Happiness increase,
> All Nature's diff'rence keeps all Nature's peace.
> Condition, circumstance is not the thing;
> Bliss is the same in subject or in king,

> *In who obtain defence, or who defend,*
> *In him who is, or him who finds a friend:*
> *Heav'n breaths thro' ev'ry member of the whole*
> *One common blessing, as one common soul.*
> *But Fortune's gifts if each alike possest,*
> *And each were equal, must not all contest?*
> *If then to all Men Happiness was meant,*
> *God in Externals could not place Content.*
> (4.49–66)

I have heard Pope's lines called smug, and they may even be viewed as an early version of *laissez-faire* or what would later pass as Social Darwinism. But I have never heard or seen an argument that Pope's lines are satiric. Yet virtually everything Mandeville says about charity schools, in another guise, is either implied or directly expressed by Pope's lines. Pope directly states that some people are, and must be, greater, richer, and wiser "than the rest"; what he doesn't say, but Mandeville does, is that "the rest" constitute most of mankind, and that many of "the rest" are not simply less wise, less great, and less rich. Many are ignorant, bestial, and poor. In short, the drift of Pope's argument is, as a *New Republic* editorial once put it, that "The Meek shall inherit the dearth." Just like Mandeville, moreover, Pope argues that the poor can be "equal in their Happiness," and somewhat like Mandeville, Pope asserts that "all Nature's diff'rence keeps all Nature's peace" because if "Fortune's gifts" were "alike possest, / And each were equal, must not all contest?" Unlike Mandeville's argument, however, Pope's arguments are enveloped in urbanity; they retain the equilibrium of a poetic fiction. His statements are poetic assertions, obviously more refined than Mandeville's in "The Grumbling Hive," and hence make little direct claim on the reader's ordinary sense of reality. If the quoted passage from Pope were flattened out into prose, as it was by Soame Jenyns, I daresay the lines would increase their capacity for controversy, though they still would not be as controversial as Mandeville's arguments.

The principal difference, however, between Mandeville and Pope is that Pope asserts order to be "Heav'n's first law." From this premise Pope elaborates his distinction between "Nature" and "Fortune," conceding Fortune to the few, though it is an "unnatural" acquisition, and reserving "Happiness" for the many, which is a natural, not to say divine, attribute. Moreover, in the poem Pope occupies the role of God's spokesman: he simply elaborates "Heav'n's first law." Mandeville, as we have seen, systematically excludes religion, though not the clergy, from his inquiry. Thus, unlike Pope, he deals exclusively with Nature, not as it is found, but as man makes it. This fundamental difference between Pope and Mandeville is clearly evident in their different methods of composition. Pope chooses to write a kind of intellectual poetic epic: his poetic statements have the appearance—the formal order—of divine truths tumbling down from heaven. Pope is a kind of messenger of God's order. Mandeville, on the other hand, is the expositor of man's order; he speaks from ground level, and correspondingly he uses the secular vehicle of plain prose. Instead of encountering Pope's beautifully articulated couplets, whose epigramatic grace virtually hypnotizes the reader into acceptance even though the couplets carry the same meaning as Mandeville's arguments, the reader of "An Essay on Charity and Charity-Schools" confronts such bald assertions as:

in a Free Nation where slaves are not allow'd of, the surest Wealth consists in a Multitude of laborious Poor. (1:287)

'Tis too much Money, excessive Wages, and unreasonable Vails that spoil servants in *England*. (1:305)

Would both Parties agree to pull off the Masque we should soon discover that whatever they pretend to, they aim at nothing so much in Charity-Schools as to strengthen their Party, and that the great Sticklers for the Church, by Educating Children in the Principles of Religion, mean inspiring them with a Superlative Veneration from the Clergy of the Church of *England*, and a strong Aversion and immortal Animosity against all that dissent from it. (1:309)

Abundance of hard and dirty Labour is to be done, and coarse Living is to be complied with: Where shall we find a better Nursery for these Necessities than the Children of the Poor? none certainly are nearer to it or fitter for it. (1:311)

Finally, Mandeville directly forces to the surface what is latent both in Pope's "heavenly" exposition of happiness and in his fearful question that "if each alike possesst, / And each were equal, must not all contest?"

To be happy is to be pleas'd, and the less Notion a Man has of a better way of Living, the more content he'll be with his own; and on the other hand, the greater a Man's Knowledge and Experience is in the World, the more exquisite the Delicacy of his Taste, and the more consummate Judge he is of things in general, certainly the more difficult it will be to please him. (1:314)

Pope lulls us into a consciousness of the law, but he reminds us that the law is sanctified by God's plan. Mandeville means to jolt us into a consciousness not just of the law but of what assumptions exist behind the law, and he instructs us that the law is man-made and designed, fundamentally, not as an expression of innate goodness, but for reasons of self-preservation. Pope attempts to create the impression that a well-ordered society is an expression of the inherent reasonableness and goodness of God's plan. Mandeville argues that a well-ordered society is a product of man's manipulation of reason, and that goodness is a form of flattery through which men are coerced into being lawful. What is perhaps most disorienting, and a principal reason why Mandeville, and not Pope, is responded to with such hostility, is that Pope believes in reason as a natural good and believes it to be God's gift to man; whereas Mandeville demonstrates reason to be a manipulatory device, a necessary fiction, to be used for what Skinner calls "cultural design."

This matter of "cultural design," and the attendant question concerning the relation between reason and goodness, is the subject of "A Search into the Nature of Society." In this essay Mandeville systematically explicates his memorable assertion that "Private Vices by the dextrous Management of a Skilful Politician may be turn'd into Publick Benefits" (1:369). This controversial formulation is the logical consequence of assumptions Mandeville makes and defends throughout "A Search into the Nature of Society." He attacks Shaftesbury because Shaftesbury "looks upon Virtue and Vice as permanent Realities that must ever be the same in all Countries and all Ages, and imagines that a Man of sound Understanding, by following the rules of Good Sense, may not only find out that *Pulchrum and Honestum* both in Morality and the Works of Art and Nature, but likewise govern himself by his Reason" (1:324). Mandeville clearly believes the notion of "Virtue and Vice as permanent Realities" to be a latent fiction. The verbal distinction between vice and virtue may itself approach permanence in human society, but the ostensible meaning to which such a distinction refers is not permanent nor innate; it is a product of human action, if not of human design. Mandeville is logically committed, as a nominalist, to resist any version of innatism or Platonism; thus he *must* challenge Shaftesbury's assumptions. In addition, Shaftesbury's notion presents Mandeville with an interesting test case: Which author, through the exercise of reason, can best explain the facts of human behavior in such a way that those facts become accessible to reason, demonstration, and verification? On purely empirical grounds Shaftesbury doesn't stand a chance, chiefly because he assumes, Platonist that he is, the limits of empiricism, whereas Mandeville argues that empiricism is all we have if we wish to exercise what is called reason.

In other parts of this essay I have mentioned Mandeville's nominalism. It is a wholly consistent linguistic and philosophical position for him to adopt since he quite clearly rejects, as he does in his discussion of Shaftesbury, any notion of universal truths. This is why Mandeville deals exclusively with the world of "is," not "ought," and why he can so confidently proclaim a position of moral relativism toward the end of "A Search into the Nature of Society": "It is in Morality as it is in Nature, there is nothing so perfectly Good in Creatures that it cannot be hurtful to any one of the Society, nor any thing so entirely Evil, but it may prove beneficial to some part or other of the Creation: So that things are only Good and Evil in reference to something else, and according to the Light and Position they are placed in" (1:367). In *The Fable of the Bees* "ought" is really "is" in disguise, and Mandeville is defending moral relativism as a hypothesis which provides us with a better description of the facts than does any hypothesis positing man's innate goodness or the permanence of vice and virtue as universal categories. With Mandeville, clearly context—rather than any ethical imperative—means everything: it is both the principal vehicle and effect of his inquiry, a fact neatly capsulized in his assertion that "Private Vices by the dextrous Management of a skilful Politician may be turn'd into Publick Benefits." [17]

Projected against a set of traditional absolutist expectations, Mandeville's argument is necessarily disorienting because its affective appeal exceeds the familiar boundaries of applied reason. But it is disorienting precisely because he raises latent assumptions to the level of conscious manipulation and thereby presents an unwelcome picture of human behavior; indeed, this is how he addresses "the force" of his reader's "prejudices." Mandeville's is a world of evolving human design, where change is absolute, where meaning is arbitrary, and where ethics, whose stability is so often assumed, is shown to be a fictional, though necessary, construction.[18] Ultimately, Mandeville's world picture is no more satiric, and no less controversial, than B. F. Skinner's view that

almost everyone makes ethical and moral judgments but this does not mean that the human species has "an inborn need or demand for ethical standards." (We could say as well that it has an inborn need or demand for unethical behavior, since almost everyone behaves unethically at some time or other.) Man has not evolved as an ethical or moral animal. He has evolved to the point at which he has constructed an ethical or moral culture. He differs from the other animals not in possessing a moral or ethical sense but in having been able to generate a moral or ethical social environment. (p. 167)

One can well understand how Mandeville's procedures and conclusions, like Skinner's, can convey the appearance of satire, chiefly because they challenge the reader's habitual ways of thinking and acting, raising latent assumptions to the level of manifest fictions. But we should also take note that Mandeville, unlike Swift or other satirists, is continually testing his premises against observable facts in accordance with the standards of rational examination. Many readers may not wish to acknowledge, or participate in, the truths of such an inquiry; but the affective appeal of the *Fable* is such that if the reader repudiates Mandeville, he does so at the risk of confessing the force of his own prejudices. For, as Mandeville shrewdly notices, "Calumny, it seems, is the shortest Way of Confuting an Adversary, when Men are touch'd in a sensible Part" (1:410).

4
Defoe, Deliverance, and Dissimulation

Many commentators have observed that Defoe has the uncanny and sometimes unsettling ability of identifying with the wide range of characters and situations he writes about—so much so that many of his works blur the literary convention of unity of point of view. Defoe's fiction has been subjected to both secular and religious readings, and the tension between these views may itself be endemic to much eighteenth-century fiction. Just a brief sampling of some recent Defoe criticism indicates both the variety of interpretations applied to his novels and the broad range of effects evidently elicited by these novels. Everett Zimmerman, for instance, has argued that "Defoe's central achievement from *Robinson Crusoe* to *Roxana* is the same: with great power and some precision, he presents characters who have been taught to assume souls but have difficulty in finding them." [1] Zimmerman further notes a dissonance between Defoe's ostensibly spiritual structures and his enactment of distinctly secular experiences; thus he argues that in *Robinson Crusoe*, "The religious structure has not resolved the psychological problem: Crusoe's story has been organized according to a traditional pattern that does not explain his behavior" (p. 35). Rather, what Zimmerman sees is that "Defoe surrounds Crusoe with fragments of meaning; the bare character is chaotic energy" (p. 44).

This "chaotic energy," to take another critical example, is precisely the interest of John J. Richetti, only he calls the energy "unmediated personal experience." [2] Like Zimmerman, Richetti senses a disjunction between secular and religious views in Defoe's fiction, but he goes on to argue that it is the function of all novelists to reveal "that process whereby experience is separated from ideology and becomes conscious of itself as the powerful if often undirected opposite of ideology" (p. 18). Thus Richetti later argues, concerning *Moll Flanders*, that "beneath the conventional language of repentance, we can easily read the language of self-assertion" (p. 136). If there is a critical consensus to be extracted from these views on the role of secular and religious experiences in Defoe's fiction, it has perhaps been most forcefully and flexibly stated by G. A. Starr, who, speaking of Defoe's use of casuistry, has observed: "It is largely by eschewing the schematic, whether in its wordly or otherwordly versions, that Defoe manages to register (if not always to resolve) so many of the moral tensions and complexities of his characters' careers." [3] In short, what Defoe does throughout his fiction is to draw the reader into the processes of thought—religious and secular—of his characters, thus decreasing the distance between the reader and the characters he ostensibly observes, because, as Starr notes, "Defoe's view of life [is] intensely problematic" (p. viii).

I use the term dissimulation, in this regard, to characterize both the authorial procedure and the problematical effects of many of Defoe's works. Defoe's dissimulation breaks down any sense of narrative distance, first, by apparently projecting the author totally into a character in order to authenticate the way that character thinks and acts, and secondly, by luring the reader not merely into observing, but participating in, the way a particular character's mind works. The cumulative effect of this procedure is that both author and reader are led into a mutual process of dissimulation whereby, voluntarily or involuntarily, we become, even if only for a moment, active participants in thoughts and actions which in our conscious life and in our conventional moral habits we might otherwise reject. Like the author, the reader becomes, if only temporarily, what Defoe's characters either are or pretend to be. In this respect, one might say that the very process of dissimulation which makes the *Shortest Way with the Dissenters*, from one point of view, a failed satire, is also the very process that enables Defoe to write his most successful fiction.

I call this process of entrapment dissimulation, rather than either imitation or ambiguity, because on the one hand I do not believe that Defoe mimetically represents characters so much as he imaginatively becomes them. Mimetic representation suggests both authorial distance and conscious control, whereas I believe Defoe neither preserves distance nor consistently exerts much authorial control. On the other hand, I do not use the term ambiguity to describe this narrative process because ambiguity suggests uncertainty among several choices. A literary work is ambiguous when a reader senses divergent possibilities of meaning and is uncertain which possibility constitutes the primary meaning. But with Defoe all meaning is primary because all experience, despite religious or ethical codes, has a claim to authenticity, and this is where I think Defoe and Richardson part company. In Defoe, the sole literary criterion of truth is experience, not correspondence to exterior perspectives or norms. Meaning is what emerges from the expression of diverse thoughts, and the truth of such meaning is left to the reader to determine, if he so chooses.

I can think of no better way of describing Defoe's authorial procedures than by briefly looking at two of his letters. In a letter to Robert Harley, Defoe advises him:

In your Perticular Post Sir you may So Govorn, as That Every Party shall believ you Their Own. . . . This is the Dissimulation I Recommend, which is Not Unlike what the Apostle Sayes of himself; becoming all Things to all Men, that he might Gain Some. This Hypocrisie is a Vertue, and by This Conduct you Shall Make your Self Popular, you shall be Faithfull and Usefull to the Soveraign and belov'd by The People.[4]

Later, acting as a secret agent for Harley, Defoe reports from Scotland:

I am Perfectly Unsuspected as Corresponding with anybody in England. I Converse with Presbyterian, Episcopall-Dissenter, papist and Non Juror, and I hope with Equall Circumspection. I flatter my Self you will have no Complaints of my Conduct. I have faithful Emissaries in Every Company And I Talk to Everybody in Their Own way. To the Merchants I am about to Settle here in Trade, Building ships & c. With the Lawyers I Want to purchase a House and Land to bring my family & live Upon it (God knows where the Money is to pay for it). To day I am Goeing into Partnership with a Membr of Parliamt in a Glass house, to morrow with Another in a Salt work. With the Glasgow Mutineers I am to be a fish Merchant, with the Aberdeen Men a woolen and with the Perth men a Linen Manufacturer, and still at the End of all Discourse the Union [of England and Scotland] is the Essentiall and I am all to Every one that I may Gain some. (*Letters*, pp. 158–59)

While two quotations do not necessarily make a case, Defoe has outlined his position in sufficient detail in the privacy of correspondence that I think we can take his dissimulation as being entirely sincere. It is tempting to attack Defoe as a hypocrite, but such an attack, as I shall argue, represents a denial of the peculiar effects that Defoe's fiction elicits from his readers. The kind of dissimulation Defoe both recommends and boasts about to Harley he clearly believes to be a "Vertue." This conviction is so strong that Defoe in both letters alludes to 1 Corinthians 9:22—"I am made all things to all men, that I might by all means save some"—in support of his own position. It is also tempting to draw from Defoe's citation of scripture the further implication that he thinks of himself and Harley as, in some sense, apostles of the public good, the public good in this case being the union of England and Scotland. From one point of view it could be argued that such a position represents a debasement of scripture, but there is no questioning the sincerity of Defoe's convictions. The virtues that devolve from his political interpretation of scripture all point to the desirability of certain public attributes: in Defoe's words, "By This Conduct you shall Make Your Self Popular, you shall be Faithfull and Usefull to the Soveraign and belov'd by The People." But these public attributes are merely the social surface of a larger private secret: the secret of dissimulation.[5]

Although it is no part of my argument that there exists a simple one-to-one relation between what Defoe says in his correspondence and what he enacts in his fiction, it is the central thesis of this chapter that the very dissimulation Defoe recommends in the two letters quoted carries over, in varying degrees and for a variety of purposes, to his fiction, and is the source of his affective appeal. This matter may be stated another way: conventional morality tends to regard dissimulation as hypocrisy, as something akin to vice, but Defoe's fiction frequently represents dissimulation as the necessary means of achieving and consolidating public success, as well as the occasion for expressing the secret desires and needs of his own readers. Defoe's dissimulating characters act out what is at least latent in the lives of many of his readers: the need to dissimulate in order to preserve secrets and the desire to know the secrets of others as they dissimulate in public life. Indeed, as Mandeville so well demonstrates, it is impossible to go through public life without dissimulation, but the dissimulation of Defoe's fiction is often made palatable to his readers, unlike the hypocrisy in Mandeville's *Fable*, because we are induced to believe that the dissimulation, once we finish the book, becomes a thing of the past. That is, through the narrative device of presenting his novels as recollections or memoirs, we are made to witness the acts of looking back

upon a period of past dissimulation, but we are similarly encouraged at
the conclusion of the novels to anticipate, if not participate in, a deliverance—perhaps providential, perhaps not—from dissimulation.

The one exception to this pattern—in its results, not in its outline—
is *Roxana*, and it is an important exception. In this work, which is in
many respects Defoe's most "modern" novel, the dissimulation never
ceases, for the process of recollection, both formally in Roxana's narrative and psychologically in the reader's experience of her narrative,
is frustrated by the denial of an anticipated resolution. The novel, in
other words, is not only about dissimulation; it *is* dissimulation, and
Roxana is condemned to her own hell. The presence of dissimulation
is made so manifest, with the sense that it is a process without end,
that many readers, expecting Defoe to follow his usual procedures of
"saving" or delivering his central character as well as his reader, have
been affronted and disoriented by the novel's rigor, and in reaction they
have attempted to sidestep the book's affective appeal by quibbling
about whether it is a finished book or whether its conclusion is at all
plausible.

Let me return, however, to the original pattern of dissimulation and
to how Defoe constructs a work so that it can (and has) become all
things to all men. When I say "constructs" I do not intend to imply
that Defoe knows at every step what he is doing; he is clearly not the
great conscious craftsman that Fielding is, but it does not follow from
this comparison that Defoe is therefore not a fine novelist. At least two
of his novels have achieved a wide audience, both in and out of the
academic community, and it seems to me valuable to try to talk about
what has made these books so popular and, in many ways, rewarding
to such a diversity of readers. Perhaps Virginia Woolf is right when she
observes about Defoe's fiction that "we find for ourselves meanings
which he was careful to disguise even from his own eye,"[6] for this
process is inevitable if Defoe's view of life is as problematic as G. A.
Starr has suggested. The diversity of interpretations of Defoe, which is
as much evidence of his ability to be "all things to all men" as it is
evidence of his readers' critical shortcomings, was well and truly
prophesied by Defoe's contemporary, Charles Gildon, when he ven-
tured to predict:

The Fabulous *Proteus* of the Ancient Mythologist was but a very faint Type of
our Hero, whose Changes are much more numerous, and he far more difficult

to be constrain'd to his own Shape. If his Works should happen to live to the next Age, there would in all probability be a greater Strife among the several Parties, whose he really was, than among the seven *Graecian* Cities, to which of them *Homer* belong'd: The *Dissenters* first would claim him as theirs, the *Whigs* in general as theirs, the *Tories* as theirs, the *Nonjurors* as theirs, the *Papists* as theirs, the *Atheists* as theirs, and so on to what Sub-divisions there may be among us.[7]

One need only mention the various and influential readings of *Robinson Crusoe* to demonstrate both how accurate Gildon's prediction is and how successfully *Robinson Crusoe* has become "all things to all men." Maximillian Novak and John Robert Moore provide important social and economic readings of *Robinson Crusoe*, G. A. Starr and J. Paul Hunter supply important religious dimensions, and Ian Watt has written a singularly influential essay on the story as a myth.[8] The question to be asked is not whether they can be all right or all wrong, for criticism, finally, is not subject to the law of the excluded middle. All these essays should be welcomed as having brought to our attention the unique and various appeals of Defoe's fiction, and it is the broad appeal of *Robinson Crusoe*, I gather, that prompted Virginia Woolf to declare about the novel that it "resembles one of the anonymous productions of the race rather than the effort of a single mind; and as for celebrating its centenary we should as soon think of celebrating the centenaries of Stonehenge itself" (*CE*, 1:62). Evidently, Defoe's singular accomplishment is to use specific events, with particular and recognizable contexts (religious, moral, social, psychological), which evoke the reader's capacity to project larger experiences and patterns of meaning on the events of the book.

If we focus for the moment on one recurrent term which weaves throughout *Robinson Crusoe*—"deliverance" (also "deliver" and "delivered")—we can see how this term may elicit diverse, and sometimes contrary, effects.[9] This term, as the *OED* demonstrates, has diverse meanings, but the principal meaning of "deliverance" is, to quote the *OED*, "The action of delivering or setting free, or fact of being set free; liberation, release, rescue." Johnson's dictionary defines deliverance as meaning, among other things, "The act of freeing from captivity, slavery, or any oppression; rescue," and Johnson goes on to cite Luke 4:18, as well as David's prayer for deliverance in Psalm 64. The important point to notice is that the term can have secular and spiritual meanings simultaneously, for unlike Richardson's *Clarissa*, *Robinson Crusoe* accommodates a variety of readers. If one is predisposed to reading *Robinson Crusoe* in light of the tradition of spiritual autobiography, then "deliverance" will mean one thing, and one will be able to trace in the novel a pattern of fall, repentance, and redemption. If, on the other hand, one is inclined toward reading the novel in light of social and economic thought, then the term will take on a different meaning. But to limit the term in either way is to deprive it of its resonance and to deny the dimensions of experience the term may elicit.

Fairly early in *Robinson Crusoe*, Robinson starts reading the Bible and comes upon Psalms 50:15—"And call upon me in the day of trouble: I will deliver thee, and thou shalt glorify me." [10] Robinson ponders the verse, initially construing deliverance as complete freedom from the island, but then it occurs to him "that I pored so much upon my deliverance from the main affliction that I disregarded the deliverance I had receiv'd . . . Have I not been deliver'd, and wonderfully too, from sickness? from the most distress'd condition that could be, and that was so frightful to me, and what notice had I taken of it? Had I done my part?" (*RC*, p. 79). Here, within the ambience of Robinson's scriptural reading, two secular meanings of the term are played against one another: deliverance as complete freedom and deliverance as a limited freedom from illness, which in turn leads Robinson to thank God for small blessings. For someone like Bunyan, deliverance points in only one direction: to the Celestial City and eternal, not secular, life. For Robinson this term is adjusted to a broad range of secular experiences within a religious context.

Robinson obsessively returns to variations on Psalms 50:15 and the notion of deliverance, both spiritual and secular. Recalling this psalm, he later reminds the reader, "How frequently in the course of our lives the evil which in it self we seek most to shun, and which, when we are fallen into it, is the most dreadful to us, is oftentimes the very means or door of our deliverance, by which alone we can be rais'd again from the affliction we are fallen into" (*RC*, p. 146)—a point that is subsequently reaffirmed when we are later told that God "does not leave his creatures so absolutely destitute but that in the worst circumstances they have always something to be thankful for, and sometimes are nearer their deliverance than they imagine; nay, are even brought to their deliverance by the means by which they seem to be brought to their destruction" (*RC*, pp. 202–203). These passages could be interpreted cynically as a version of sinning your way to heaven, or as a version of the paradox of the fortunate fall, or as an example of the short-sightedness of man, or as a statement of reassurance to the reader that we are all sinful but, with patience and a good heart, we will all eventually be delivered from our present afflictions.

It is this last sense of reassurance—at once secular and religious— which eventually dominates the last pages of the novel, for the reader, like Robinson, will be "saved" by Defoe. The reader, one could sur-mise, is a person who has known a sense of sin or guilt or anxiety and who, in a penitential state of mind, has yearned for deliverance, be it secular or spiritual, both witnesses and participates in Robinson's liberation from an extended period of isolation (twenty-eight years, two months, and nineteen days, to be exact). Moreover, it is fascinating to observe how Robinson responds to the captain who rescues him from the island; for the captain, in accordance with the multiple uses of deliverance, simultaneously appears as a secular presence and a spiritual vehicle of deliverance:

Then I took my turn, and embrac'd him as my deliverer; and we rejoyc'd together. I told him I look upon him as a man sent from heaven to deliver me, and that the whole transaction seemed to be a chain of wonders; that such things as these were the testimonies we had of a secret hand of Providence governing the world, and an evidence that the eyes of an infinite power could search into the remotest corner of the world, and send help to the miserable whenever he pleased. (*RC*, p. 219)

This is an expression of the most reassuring form of dissimulation, for the passage clearly evokes both a secular and a religious meaning with perfect equanimity, and thereby adjusts itself to a variety of readers. Such reassurance, I might add, is antithetical to Richardson's under-standing of deliverance, and it points to a major difference between Richardson's and Defoe's understanding of religion, as I shall argue in the next chapter.

In fact, however, the most magnificent act of dissimulation in this passage may be that it is neither the captain nor God whom we finally sense as the agent of Providence. As Homer Brown has suggested, "While Defoe is impersonating Robinson Crusoe, he is also imperson-ating on another level Providence itself."[11] That is, he is himself the author of a "chain of wonders" which are as well testimonies of his

"secret hand of Providence governing the world." Obviously all novelists are in some respect providential since they can control their characters' fate and determine the outcome of their story. But what I am suggesting is that in *Robinson Crusoe*, and to a lesser extent in *Moll
Flanders*, *Captain Singleton*, and *Colonel Jack*, Defoe himself, mainly
through his remarkable conclusions, either imitates or becomes the in-
visible hand of God, and thereby "delivers" his readers, just as he
saves his characters. I would further suggest that many readers intuitive-
ly sense this to be Defoe's basic appeal, and thus they come to expect
a mysterious deliverance to occur at the end of Defoe's novels (including *Journal of the Plague Year*, even if it is not regarded as a novel).
The expectation of deliverance is frustrated once—in *Roxana*—and I
would say this is a sure sign that here Defoe abandons his providential
role as a deliverer, just as he abandons Roxana to her own agonizing
fate.

What Moll Flanders seeks, for example, is precisely what Robinson originally abandoned and took twenty-eight years to recover: the
middle state of life, where one satisfies both secular and spiritual
needs.[12] Moll tell us: "I knew what I aim'd at, and what I wanted,
but knew nothing how to pursue the End by direct means; I wanted to
be placed in a settled State of Living, and had I happen'd to meet with
a sober good Husband, I should have been as faithful and true a Wife
to him as Virtue it self could have form'd: If I had been otherwise,
the Vice came in always at the Door of Necessity, not at the Door of
Inclination" (*MF*, p. 101). But Moll is unlike Robinson in two important respects, which in turn point to her defense and need of dissimulation. Robinson frequently attributes his own conduct to "a meer
wandring inclination" (*RC*, p. 6), and he further asserts that "I was
under no necessity of seeking my bread" (*RC*, p. 71). Moll, on the
other hand, says she is moved by necessity, not by inclination. Now we
need not believe Moll totally to appreciate that the novel works somewhat differently from *Robinson Crusoe*. Even if Moll is moved by
necessity, it is clear that many of her actions delight both her and her
reader's inclinations, but more of this later when we examine the novel's
preface. The point is that Moll in this passage is building up a case for
dissimulation (i.e., other than "direct means") on the grounds that she
is a woman, and she is justifying her dissimulation as a means to
achieve the very middle state Robinson rejected.

As a woman in a male-dominated society, Moll is just as isolated as Robinson on the island. She does not enjoy the social reassurance that would be provided 250 years later by the woman's movement. To this extent, Moll's isolation would and should have considerable resonance for her female readers. But Moll also has the capacity, like Robinson, to be all things to all men, for her use of dissimulation to achieve "a settled State of Living" represents a desire that many readers both know and share. What is more remarkable about Moll is that she does not simply state her case abstractly; rather, she turns the fact of her isolation into an instrument—possibly of casuistry—to implicate the reader in her own dissimulation.[13] She turns to the reader as her confidant, and if, after hearing her out, we read on, then we have tacitly endorsed her actions:

I found by experience, that to be Friendless is the worst Condition, next to being in want that a Woman can be reduc'd to: *I say a Woman*, because 'tis evident Men can be their own Advisers, and their own Directors, and know how to work themselves out of Difficulties and into Business better than Women; but if a Woman has no Friend to Communicate her Affairs to, and to advise and assist her, 'tis ten to one but she is undone; nay, and the more Money she has, the more Danger she is in of being wrong'd and deceiv'd. . . . In the next place, when a Woman is thus left desolate and void of Council, she is just like a Bag of Money, or a Jewel dropt on the Highway, which is a Prey to the next Comer; if a Man of Virtue and upright Principles happens to find it, he will have it cried [advertised], and the Owner may come to hear of it again; but how many times shall such a thing fall into Hands that will make no scruple of seizing it for their own, to once that it shall come into good Hands. (*MF*, pp. 100–101)

I have already remarked on how Moll implicates the reader as her sympathetic confidant. But even if we are not sympathetic, this passage forestalls any attempt the reader might make to put some distance between himself and Moll. Moll forces a recognition of her condition on the reader. She is alone in at least two respects: she is without friends, and, as a woman, she is isolated in a male-dominated society. But she turns her apparent social weakness as a woman into an affective strength as she deals with her reader. That is, insofar as this passage is directed to men she uses her vulnerability as a woman as the occasion for flattering male social prowess: "'Tis evident Men can be their own advisers, and their own Directors, and know how to work themselves out of Difficulties and into Business better than Women." But what is this special knowledge that males possess? Social power certainly, but is not social power frequently exercised through dissimulation? Harley and Defoe know so, and I suspect the reader does as well. This mutual awareness of dissimulation between the reader and Moll is still further underscored by her comments on money. Money alone will not solve Moll's problems, for "the more Money she has, the more Danger she is in of being wrong'd and deceiv'd." Wronged and deceived by whom? If men dominate social and political power, it follows that men are more likely to wrong and deceive a woman; in short, the bond of dissimulation is tightened still more, and the male reader must at least recognize what she is saying, even if he chooses not to be implicated.

This appeal is directed to the reader's own observations and experiences—to the reader's own use of dissimulation—and we are even provided with a test by which we can estimate our own position with respect to Moll's arguments. What would we do if we happened upon a bag of money or a jewel dropped on the highway? Would we keep it or return it? Granting the possibility of the latter, Moll nevertheless suggests the probability of the former. In keeping with Defoe's use of dissimulation, this test grows out of a perplexing analogy: that is, if Moll in her present condition is like a bag of money or a jewel, then the question becomes, Whose hands will she fall into—both within and without the novel? What will the reader do with her? The analogy suggests that Moll, though presently discarded, is valuable. What is her value, and what is implied about the reader's understanding of her value in the tantalizing sentence, "But how many times shall such a thing fall into Hands that will make no scruple of seizing it for their own, to once that it shall come into good Hands?" Isn't it possible for something to be seized as our own and yet fall into "good Hands?" Seeing this question in relation to Moll's later summation of the moral of her history and the preface to the novel will illumine Moll's relationship to the reader and the larger affective appeal of the novel.

Toward the end of the novel, Moll summarizes the value of her recollections in this way: "The Moral indeed of all my History is left to be gather'd by the Senses and Judgment of the Reader; I am not Qualified to preach to them, let the Experience of one Creature compleatly Wicked, and compleatly Miserable be a Storehouse of useful warning to those that read" (*MF*, p. 210). Few readers, so far into the novel, believe that Moll is either "compleatly Wicked" or "compleatly

Miserable." She is not completely wicked because the more we know about any person—the more information we accumulate about a person's past (and we certainly know a lot about Moll's past)—the more difficult it is to pass the inflexible judgment of wickedness on him. Moreover, because the reader is implicated by Moll's dissimulation he is likely to temper his judgments on the prudent grounds that he knows the complexities of his own motives and is not about to condemn himself without qualification. Nor is Moll completely miserable, though she surely knows misery. She is too energetic, too alive, to be completely miserable. Does it then follow that Moll is a liar in this and similar passages, or that Defoe is being ironic? I think not. This passage is an instance of her (and Defoe's) dissimulation in the sense that the meaning of the passage points in several directions. Moll's seeming condemnation of herself satisfies any moral inclination to judge her according to conventional ethical standards; in a sense she disarms us with her candor. But at the same time the cumulative effect of her experiences severely qualifies the usefulness or applicability of such detached standards. This is a classic example of how Defoe's characters, as Everett Zimmerman has argued, "present their own cases and demand our sympathy. We are not put in the position of detached observers who overlook the instructive collapse of a puppet." [14]

Moreover, this dissimulation with the reader is suggested by the distinction Moll makes between "the Senses and Judgment of the Reader." "Judgment" may refer to the reader's use of reason and observation, but it can also refer to the moral tendency either to approve or condemn an action. "Sense" could refer to good sense or common sense, but Moll uses the plural form "Senses," which suggests to me that she is alluding to how we feel about her, how we experience her. In this reading, judgment and sense, or the tendency to evaluate abstractly as distinguished from experiencing emotionally, may well come into conflict, and I daresay many readings of *Moll Flanders*, as well as readings of other works of Defoe, tend to veer between sympathy and judgment, to use G. A. Starr's useful distinction. [15] The reader hesitates between the apparent poles of judgment and sympathy, observation and participation, and he is left in this condition because, like Moll, he emotionally feels the need for dissimulation, though he may abstractly disapprove of it.

This reading receives considerable impetus from the novel's preface, which acts as a paradigm of the reader's subsequent experience of the novel. At the heart of this paradigm is the implication that the reader, like Moll, is both familiar with and an agent of dissimulation:

> What is left 'tis hop'd will not offend the chastest Reader or the modestest Hearer; and as the best use is made even of the worst story, the Moral 'tis hop'd will keep the Reader serious even where the story might incline him to be otherwise: To give the History of a wicked life repented of, necessarily requires that the wicked Part should be made as wicked as the real History of it will bear, to illustrate and give a Beauty to the Penitent part, which is certainly the best and brightest, if related with equal Spirit and Life.
>
> It is suggested there cannot be the same Life, the same Brightness and Beauty, in relating the Penitent Part, as is in the Criminal Part: If there is any Truth in that Suggestion, I must be allow'd to say, 'tis because there is not the same taste and relish in the Reading, and indeed it is too true that the difference lyes not in the real worth of the Subject so much as in the Gust and Palate of the Reader.
>
> But as this work is chiefly recommended to those who know how to Read it, and how to make the good Uses of it, which the Story all along recommends to them, so it is to be hop'd that such Readers will be much more pleas'd with the Moral than the fable, with the Application than with the Relation, and with the End of the Writer than with the Life of the Person written of. (*MF*, pp. 3–4)

The preface is both an instance of, and a stimulus to employ, semantic juggling. Verbally, as well as psychologically, the whole passage is built on dissimulation. If we focus on the distinctions established in this passage, we can see how, individually and collectively, they not only express paradoxes but cumulatively induce a kind of mental paralysis, where the process of rational observation is overtaxed with distinctions. That is, how many distinctions can a rational reader sustain simultaneously? How many terms can the reader juggle before he loses his grip? We are told that the "best use" may be made of the "worst story," that the "Moral" may keep the reader "serious," even if the "story" might incline us to be "otherwise," that the "wicked Part," if it is to be authentic, must be really wicked, but the "Penitent part" will have the greater "Beauty"; but if the reader should prefer the wicked part, it is not the writer's fault—it is the fault of "the Gust and Palate of the Reader." Assuming that all readers, to varying extents, possess a gust and palate, we are nevertheless cautioned that this book is chiefly recommended to those "who know how to Read it, and how to make the good Uses of it," and presumably those readers who know how to read the book properly will be more pleased with (and capable of sustaining throughout the novel) the following distinctions: the "Moral" rather than the "Fable," the "Application" rather than the "Relation," the "End of the Writer" rather than the "Life of the Person written of." Such distinctions are a virtual parody of what I call the impossible observer.

This passage has it all ways and in fact meshes well with Moll's dissimulation and her ability to implicate the reader. Like Moll's analogy of the bag of money and jewel, the passage creates problems in the guise of providing solutions to them. It is possible, abstractly, to sustain all the distinctions contained in the preface. But we might also remember what Kierkegaard said about abstract thought: it is thought without a thinker. Defoe can tell us abstractly how to read his book, but he cannot control how we experience it, especially when his novel is so evocative. He knows very well that the gust and palate of the reader will largely determine his response to the novel, and it is precisely Moll's gust and palate—her ability to experience and to stimulate experiences in her readers, rather than her thoughts, which are barely disguised platitudes—which have endeared her to so many readers. The distinctions so well summarized in the preface are, finally, not exclusive but inclusive, and this is what makes reading *Moll Flanders* such a satisfying, albeit morally perplexing, experience.[16] The reader, to use Moll's analogy, can both make no scruple of seizing her experience for his own and at the same time assure himself, as Moll and Defoe assure us, that she does "come into good Hands"—for an ostensibly moral purpose.

It is precisely this ability to enact, evaluate, and absorb all these distinctions that characterizes the dissimulation of *Moll Flanders*. The dissimulation I have been examining is not simply a matter of literary ambiguity, though ambiguity is certainly a part of it. Ambiguity, in my view, functions as a device for expressing either uncertainty or diversity, both of which appear in Defoe's fiction. Defoe's dissimulation in *Moll Flanders* and *Robinson Crusoe*, however, is not merely a manipulated device, but an inclusive vision stimulating within the reader thoughts and feelings that transcend or break apart the conventional categories of morality and society at the same time that these categories appear to be sustained. Defoe's fiction can be all things to all men only so long as it stimulates, but eventually resists, the reader's urge to make it into some one thing for some one person. To borrow a distinction from Virginia Woolf, Defoe's dissimulation is most effective when it gives the reader a sense of both "the freedom of fiction" (i.e., the ability to participate imaginatively in an experience) and "the substance of fact" (i.e., the reassurance of detached observation) (*CE*, 4:234). But the tendency of *Robinson Crusoe* and *Moll Flanders* to resolve themselves by having it both ways is not characteristic of *Roxana*, whose massive inclusiveness impedes, for several reasons, Defoe's customary sense of deliverance.

The inclusiveness and dissimulation of *Roxana*, unlike those of *Robinson Crusoe* and *Moll Flanders*, do not lead toward deliverance— secular or spiritual—either for Roxana or the reader. They lead toward progressive concealment, frustration, and disillusionment. Step by step, Defoe leads Roxana and the reader up the rungs of the social ladder, only, paradoxically, to guide her and us to the bottom of our souls. This dual process, which is an extension of Defoe's dissimulation, should not be mistaken for inconsistency. Rather, as G. A. Starr has argued, we should recall that "elsewhere in his writings, Defoe quotes approvingly the apostolic principle of being all things to all men so as to gain some, and a good bit of the inconsistency in what Roxana says of herself might be regarded as Pauline doctrine put into bizarre but effective practice." [17]

One way of looking at this dual process in *Roxana* is to examine the way the work methodically exhausts the possibilities and conventions of Defoe's earlier novels. While our sympathy is enlisted for Roxana early in the book, and contempt is elicited in the later stages, neither response represents an adequate estimate of the novel's divergent effects. This novel, unlike any of the others, presents not just the public, but the psychic, unfolding of the total range of experience of Roxana's life. In fact, Roxana initially oscillates between the claims of public and private life, but as she progressively retreats from public life, disguising herself as a wealthy widow, a Quaker, and a countess, the novel withdraws into the inner terror of her mind, where public disguise and masquerading are merely the social surface of the psychological compulsion to dissimulate. This process of progressive internalization, in effect, represents a recapitulation, reexamination, and extension of the conventions that serve Defoe so well in *Robinson Crusoe* and *Moll Flanders*.

The reader's initial sympathy, as G. A. Starr has shown, is aroused when Roxana is deserted by her husband and left with five children. She is penniless, at the point of starvation, and Defoe underscores the sense of pity through his scriptural references to Job 2:11-13 and Lamentations 2:20. Roxana aptly observes that "the Truth was, there was no Need of much Discourse in the Case, the Thing spoke itself." [18] The early enlistment of pity somewhat mitigates the reader's attitude toward Roxana's first adulterous relationship, for there is a sense in which Roxana enters this affair out of necessity (to use one of Defoe's favorite terms). At this point Defoe suggests, moreover, that Roxana is not only vulnerable to, but in part victimized by, both her loyal servant, Amy, and the landlord, who knows a ripe opportunity when he sees one. To this extent, Roxana's initial downfall appears to grow out of the same conventional formula about poverty that informs *Moll Flanders:*

But Poverty was my Snare; dreadful Poverty! The Misery I had been in, was great, such as wou'd make the Heart tremble at the Apprehensions of its Return; and I might appeal to any that has had any Experience of the World, whether one so entirely destitute as I was, of all manner of all Helps, or Friends, either to support me, or to assist me to support myself, could withstand the Proposal [of adultery]; not that I plead this as a Justification of my Conduct, but that it may move the Pity, even of those that abhor the Crime. (*R*, p. 39)

This passage strikes a delicate balance: Roxana may not be pleading for justification, but the very mention of her condition is calculated to elicit the reader's sympathy. It all looks like a repetition of *Moll Flanders*, but it isn't. The countermovement in this early section, which qualifies but does not necessarily discredit Roxana's dread of poverty, is represented by her loyal servant and friend, Amy (*ami*). Amy grows out of another convention that Defoe has earlier put to use in his other novels: the trusted friend and confidant, be it Robinson's Friday, Moll's houselady, Singleton's William Walters, or Colonel Jack's sidekick, Will, or his tutor in America. Thus the temptation is strong to view Amy as just another repetition of a convention, but she isn't. Amy, who is one of Defoe's greatest dissimulators, not only serves Roxana; she also mirrors her social and psychological condition and, most important, acts out her will. Amy is at once individual and collective instinct; she represents Roxana's antisocial inclinations, her aggressive assertion of self, and her concomitant terror of the consequences of her social defiance. Amy is, as Roxâna frequently reminds us, resolute, as well as possessed of tremendous managerial skill, and she is specifically associated with the devil. Discussing with Roxana the impending adul-

terous affair which Roxana initially denies will occur, Amy warns
Roxana, "I'd do anything to get you out of this sad Condition; as to
Honesty, I think Honesty is out of the Question, when Starving is the
Case" (*R*, p. 28). But Roxana, ignoring Amy's opinion of "Honesty,"
seemingly tries to counter Amy's advice when she apparently chides
her: "But that I know you to be a very honest Girl, *Amy, says I*, you
wou'd make me abhor you; why, you argue for the Devil, as if you
were one of his Privy-Counsellors" (*R*, p. 37).

The reason for my hesitating use of "seemingly" and "apparently"
is that it is not clear whether Roxana at this point does not believe
Amy, is ignoring what Amy has said, or is dissimulating with Amy and
the reader. This point is crucial, not just for understanding Roxana's
subsequent affair with the landlord, but because Roxana eventually
speaks this way when Amy, at the end of the novel, both proposes
and apparently carries out the murder of Roxana's daughter. The question of complicity—social, legal, and psychological—represents a new
dimension of Defoe's use and examination of dissimulation, and the
reader must be sensitive to this question in order to reconcile the seeming inconsistencies of Roxana's explanation of how and why she entered
into the adulterous relationship:

Had I consulted Conscience and Virtue, I shou'd have repell'd this *Amy*, how-
ever faithful and honest to me in other things, as a Viper, and Engine of the
Devil; I ought to have remembered that neither he or I, either by the Laws of
God or Men, cou'd come together, upon any other Terms than that of notorious
Adultery: The ignorant Jade's Argument, That he had brought me out of
the Hands of the Devil, by which she meant the Devil of Poverty and Dis-
tress, shou'd have been a powerful Motive to me, not to plunge myself into the
Jaws of Hell, and into the Power of the real Devil, in Recompence for that
Deliverence. (*R*, p. 38)

This passage may be read as Roxana's condemnation of Amy for
persuading her into victimization, but such a reading is difficult to
sustain. It is also possible to read the passage as Roxana's fear of the
real persuasiveness of Amy's appeal. That is, Amy has argued soundly,
but Roxana detests the conclusion. Again it is possible to read the passage as Roxana's grudging and terrifying recognition that Amy's arguments have drawn out and enacted Roxana's latent inclination, an inclination which Roxana, when she is no longer a victim of necessity,
later poses as a question: "*What was I a Whore for Now?*" (*R*, p. 201).

Roxana says she should have repelled "this Amy," which is an interesting usage; for she (and Defoe) could easily have said just "Amy." The French meaning of "friend" is obvious, and I suppose one could argue that Roxana uses the name sarcastically. But Roxana does not abandon Amy, just as despite her declarations, she does not abandon Amy after the apparent murder. Indeed, Amy's "punishment" for her complicity in the adulterous affair is that Roxana forces her to go to bed with the landlord—an action characteristic of the novel's unconventional effects. At critical points where rational observation would demand that the characters pull back from an experience, the novel instead pushes ahead and makes the reader participate in more bizarre experiences. To put it another way, Defoe plunges not just Roxana, but the reader, into "the Jaws of Hell," from which there will be no "Deliverance."

Just as Defoe complicates the convention of necessity in the first part of the novel, so Roxana's second affair with the prince, which represents a rise up the social ladder now that she is wealthy, tantalizes us with another set of conventions appropriate to her inclinations. As Roxana says, "Tho' Poverty and Want is an irresistible Temptation to the Poor, Vanity and Great Things are as irresistable to others" (*R*, p. 64). But we should not be deceived by Roxana's seeming honesty, nor should we accept her view that her affair in France makes her "a standing Mark of the Weakness of Great Men, in their Vice" (*R*, p. 74). To do so would be to accept the prince's judgment that no one but Roxana has "such Skin, without Paint, in the World" (*R*, p. 72). Roxana's "Paint" is not conspicuous, because it is like a clear veneer: we must look through the novel's social surface to its moral and psychological effects. Her affair with the prince is used as a social and conventional instrument by which Defoe examines Roxana as she acquires wealth, and this section or stage of her life is clearly marked out when Defoe has Roxana say: "Now I was become, from a Lady of Pleasure, a Woman of Business, and of great Business too, I assure you" (*R*, p. 131).

What happens in this section and in the subsequent sections at the English court is that Roxana translates her sexual inclinations into the acquisition and manipulation of wealth. She is not motivated, like Moll, Singleton, or Colonel Jack, by a desire to remove herself from necessity and to achieve a settled state of life. Again Defoe widens a prior convention: Roxana uses wealth and sex to exercise her will and to

manipulate and consume others with raw power. Her distinction between "Pleasure" and "Business" is both merged and obliterated by
her devouring will, as we can see in her report of her conversation
with the Dutch merchant: "I that was infinitely oblig'd to him before,
began to talk to him as if I had ballanc'd Accounts with him now; and
that the Favour of Lying with a Whore, was equal, not to the thousand
Pistoles only, but to all the Debt I ow'd him, for saving my Life, and
all my Effects" (*R*, p. 144). Roxana is here talking to a man who both
delivered her from danger in Paris and who now lawfully wishes to
marry her. Although Roxana's comments may be ungracious, the horror
of the exchange lies in the phrase "ballanc'd Accounts." Roxana
willingly acknowledges that she is a high-class whore, that she believes
she has paid off all debts, but in doing so she has transformed human
feeling, associated with sexuality, into a mercantile abstraction, the
mere exchange of commodities. This is no longer a simple matter, say,
of Moll Flanders's abundant energy, for Moll, unlike Roxana, continues throughout her narrative to experience pleasure. In the guise of
advancing what looks to be a precursor of the modern argument for
woman's rights, Roxana is dissimulating something more, something
latent in her will which she can express but which she can never fully
acknowledge and assimilate: "I return'd, that While a Woman was
single, she was a Masculine in her politick Capacity; that she had then
the full Command of what she had, and the full Direction of what she
did; that she was a Man in her separated Capacity, to all Intents and
Purposes that a Man cou'd be so to himself; that she was controul'd
by none, because Accountable to none, and was in Subjection to none"
(*R*, pp. 148–49).

     As I have said, it is tempting to see this passage as an anticipation
of woman's rights, just as it might be tempting to view it as a logical
extension of Moll Flanders's earlier observations on the roles of men
and women in society. On a political level Roxana's arguments have a
singularly modern appeal: she is arguing for equality, for human rights.
But the political level of Roxana's argument conceals a larger psychological compulsion to dissimulate: Roxana does not just desire equal
rights—she wants to be a man, or her version of a man, and not just
in a political sense.[19] She has successfully used her sexuality to acquire
wealth, she has merged her sexuality with wealth (her model man is
Sir Robert Clayton, investment counselor at large), and now she takes

pleasure in manipulating her wealth in the same way, and with the same energy, that one achieves sexual satisfaction.

This desire to be a man in the guise of a woman represents a totally new dimension of Defoe's dissimulation. The affective appeal of such a desire is troubling, for it not only represents a disorienting use of narrative conventions but generates a sense of trauma which is never, and probably never could be, resolved. Roxana says, "And now I began to act in a new Sphere" (*R*, p. 172), meaning that she has moved further up the social ladder to the court, but her actions at court also represent a new sphere of experience, where her perverse inclinations · directly implicate the highest levels of English society. Masquerading at court is, of course, an appropriate vehicle for Roxana's translation of sexual roles. Her famous Turkish dance at court, where she gains the name of Roxana, elicits the same blend of fascination and disgust that the British film *The Ruling Class* reveals and mocks in British aristocracy. Concerning this dance and the widespread sense of perversity throughout the novel Michael Shinagel has remarked:

Without question Defoe's imagination . . . was beginning to dwell on the perverse side of life, and he probably was disturbed by it. Consider the unexplained and erotic scene where Roxana forces her faithful maid to lie with the landlord. . . . Such incidents as this or Roxana's lascivious Turkish dance or even the dark guilt-ridden atmosphere Defoe manages to generate in the closing yet inconclusive pages of the story, where the murder of a daughter is plotted and perhaps executed, all these revealing signs suggest, in short, that Defoe no longer was able to control his imagination or his material.[20]

The very approach-avoidance conflict evident in Shinagel's observations indicates the peculiar effects of Defoe's dissimulation on the reader. It is a dissimulation that enacts and stimulates not merely eroticism generally, but the latent erotic basis of social conventions. The dissimulation of *Roxana* is such that by its very inability to be controlled—by Defoe, Roxana, or the reader—the novel generates the capacity to be all things to all men. It is all things because once the reader's erotic imagination is stimulated he will project his own latent fantasies on the events and language of the novel. The reader will see what he ordinarily represses, and he will respond to what he sees with varying degrees of recognition and varying acknowledgments of complicity. Shinagel calls the scene with Amy and the landlord "unexplained," but I have suggested that it is artistically and psychologically plausible. Shinagel refers to Roxana's "lascivious Turkish dance," but the passage about Roxana's dance reads as follows: "I danc'd by Myself a Figure which I learnt in *France*, when the Prince *de*—— desir'd I wou'd dance for his Diversion; it was indeed, a very fine Figure, invented by a famous Master at *Paris*, for a Lady or a Gentleman to dance single; but being perfectly new, it pleas'd the Company exceedingly, and they all thought it had been *Turkish*" (*R*, p. 175).

Strictly speaking, the dance is neither lascivious nor Turkish; but the scene of masquerading, and the stimulus of the word "Turkish," have the ability to elicit erotic projections from the reader, projections that evidently disturb Shinagel. The dance itself, seen in the guise of *Roxana* dissimulating her latent masculinity (she dances alone) through conspicuously feminine dress and gesture, could just as easily be viewed as Roxana's celebration of her own personal and social defiance. The point is not, finally, whether Shinagel is right or I am, nor is it just a case of Defoe not being able "to control his imagination." Rather, the materials of the novel are so stimulating—its affective appeal is so strong—that the reader has trouble controlling *his* imagination.

Several critics have, in a variety of ways, drawn attention to the psychological complexity of *Roxana*, though they have not spoken about how the novel stimulates the reader's erotic imagination. Robert Hume has observed that "the reader is not allowed to stand off and coolly watch Roxana's agonies. Instead he is thrust into her perplexed condition and left to flounder." Everett Zimmerman speaks of Roxana's "confused mind that does not fully comprehend either its own stratagems or difficulties"; and Maximillian Novak has argued that "the final section of the novel reflects Defoe's growing interest in psychology."[21] Where I disagree with Novak, in particular, is in his assertion that "what prevents *Roxana* from being Defoe's masterpiece is the truncated ending" (p. 464). The ending appears truncated because, contrary to his practice in the other novels, Defoe provides no resolution to Roxana's dissimulation. But the conclusion of *Roxana* is peculiar in another, more important respect. There are two conclusions to *Roxana:* the first concludes the formal narrative and the chronological extent of Roxana's recollections, on page 265; the second, at the end of the novel, charts Roxana's terror—religious, moral, and psychological—and encourages the reader's participation in a distinctively unorthodox manner.

I began this discussion by remarking on the novel's dual movement: Roxana's progressive rise up the social ladder and her progressive descent into terror. By page 265 Roxana has married the Dutch merchant, has amassed enormous wealth, and has achieved the status of a countess in Holland. In short, she has socially accomplished her highest point. If this were *Moll Flanders*, *Captain Singleton*, or *Colonel Jack*, the novel would be over. But Defoe defies his prior conventions, and Roxana explicitly signals the widening of this convention: "I must now go back to another Scene, and join it to this End of my Story" (*R*, p. 265). In other words, the reader will experience a second conclusion. This second conclusion represents a new psychological dimension in Defoe's fiction. Ordinarily, as I have observed, Defoe's fiction is constructed around a movement of recollection and anticipation. The narrator recollects a dissimulating past, but the conclusion to the recollection projects both the reader's deliverance from, and anticipated cessation of, dissimulation. But in *Roxana* Defoe resists this use of recollection and denies both to Roxana and the reader the pleasure of an anticipated resolution. Instead, within the unfolding of Roxana's recollections, he introduces a second and deeper level of psychological inquiry, and it is this deepened inquiry into the story of Roxana's two daughters that occurs between the first and second conclusions. Instead of moving forward in time from the first conclusion on page 265, the story moves backward and deeper into time. Instead of ascending toward an external social resolution, the novel descends into Roxana's tormented mind.

Just after Roxana has been married to the Dutch merchant, which is the first conclusion of the novel, she learns from Amy that her daughter Susan (this is also Roxana's real first name), may now know that Roxana is her mother. Several things have thus happened at once which give this section tremendous psychological resonance. It is, first of all, Roxana who initiated the inquiry into her daughters' lives; it is Amy, the trusted friend and servant, who has enacted Roxana's will to discover a distant part of her past. The fact that Roxana's first name is the same as her daughter's suggests that Defoe knowingly, or instinctively, is working with a form of psychological doubling— and the doubling might be viewed as tripling, if one views Amy as both the social and psychological instrument and expression of Roxana's will. The sense of psychological tripling is further complicated because Susan first thinks that Amy is her mother. Without suggesting that I can work out the complications of Defoe's psychological interests, I simply call attention to their peculiar effects and to the extraordinary operations the reader must perform in response to the complexity of this section. The dissimulation is not merely technical but experiential, as we can see, first, in Roxana's reaction to Amy's proposal of murder, and second, in her response to her own daughter, who, though she is not certain that Roxana is her mother, talks about Roxana's Turkish dress in the presence of the disguised Roxana.

Amy was so provok'd, that she told me, *in short*, she began to think it would be absolutely necessary to murther her: That Expression fill'd me with Horror: all my Blood ran chill in my Veins, and a Fit of trembling seiz'd me, that I cou'd not speak a good-while; at last, What is the Devil in you, *Amy, said I?* Nay, nay, *says She*, let it be the Devil, or not the Devil, if I thought she knew one tittle of your History, I wou'd dispatch her if she were my own Daughter a thousand times; and I, *says I in a Rage*, as well as I love you, wou'd be the first that shou'd put the Halter about your Neck, and see YOU hang'd . . . nay, *says I*, you wou'd not live to be hang'd, *I believe*, I shou'd cut your Throat with my own Hand; I am almost ready to do it, *said I*, as 'tis, for your but naming the thing. . . . (*R*, pp. 270–71)

What my Face might do towards betraying me, I know not, because I cou'd not see myself, but my Heart beat as if it wou'd have jump'd out at my Mouth; and my Passion was so great, that for want of Vent, I thought I shou'd have burst: . . . I had no Vent; no-body to open myself to, or to make a Complaint to for my Relief; I durst not leave the Room by any means, for then she wou'd have told all the Story in my Absence, and I shou'd have been perpetually uneasie to know what she had said, or had not said; so that, *in a word*, I was oblig'd to sit and hear her tell all the Story of *Roxana, that is to say*, of myself, and not know at the same time, whether she was in earnest or in jest; whether she knew me or no; or, *in short*, whether I was to be expos'd or not expos'd. (*R*, pp. 284–85)

   The levels of dissimulation and complexity in these two passages are fairly easy to sense but extremely difficult to discuss and assess. Roxana's anger with Amy is clearly and deliberately an echo of her much earlier anger with Amy's assessment of the landlord's motives. Once again Amy is likened to the devil, but it is well to recall that she is Roxana's servant. Moreover, when Roxana finally suspects that the murder has occurred she neither has Amy hanged nor cuts her throat. Roxana's anger, in fact, seems less directed at the fact of murder, than at Amy's "naming the thing." The act of "naming" specifies, particu-

larizes, and raises to consciousness what Roxana wishes to leave obscure and latent. Here again Amy seems to function as the psychological enactment of Roxana's will. Roxana projects, but never explicitly
names, certain desires, and Amy intuits and enacts them. In this respect
Roxana is more terrified by the exposure of her own desires than by
Amy's subsequent enactment of them. Amy is, to borrow a term from
the second passage, Roxana's "Vent." Amy projects and purges
Roxana's will, but she does not, and finally cannot, resolve her mis-
tress's tentative movement toward self-destruction. Whatever the case,
Roxana's recollections are not, for her or the reader, therapeutic. They
are traumatic.

This capacity to stimulate the reader's conjecture and projection,
and yet frustrate the desire for resolution, is appropriate to the novel's
dissimulation. The reader, like Roxana, wants to know: like her, we
feel obliged to sit and hear "the Story of *Roxana*," and like her we
are fascinated by the compulsive tension between exposure and concealment. We are never completely sure how much has been exposed
and concealed, and in this way the novel stimulates our desires but
never fully satisfies them. One critic has suggested that there are two
Roxanas: "a changing, experiencing character who tends to excuse and
defend her actions and an evaluating narrator who is often repulsed by
her earlier actions." [22] But perhaps a prayer in Defoe's correspondence
(which also appears in *Colonel Jack*) is more helpful in isolating the
traumatic effect of the novel:

> *Lord, whatsoever Troubles wrack my Breast*
> *Till Sin removes too, let me take no Rest;*
> *How dark soe'er my Case, or sharp my Pain,*
> *O let no Sorrows cease, and Sin remain!*
> *For JESUS Sake, remove not my Distress*
> *Till thy Almighty Grace shall repossess*
> *The vacant Throne, from whence my Crimes depart,*
> *And makes a willing Captive of my Heart.*
> (*Letters*, p. 449)

Defoe's comment on the prayer illumines the novel's unconventional conclusion and Roxana's extraordinary condition: "Its a prayer, I
doubt few can make: But the Moral is excellent; if Afflictions cease,
and Cause of Afflictions remain, the Joy of your Deliverance will be

short." There are many Roxanas because her afflictions, as well as their causes, are themselves manifold and problematical. The end of the novel feels formally truncated, though it is affectively expansive, because there can be no "deliverance" for a character who has been aptly called "Defoe's only damned soul."[24]

5
'Clarissa,' 'Amelia,' and the State of Probation

It has frequently been noted that *Amelia* represents Fielding's altered conception of the novel, especially in light of his understanding of *Clarissa*.[1] However, my discussion of *Amelia* and *Clarissa* will focus less on the question of influence than on how Richardson and Fielding, using such common thematic interests as the trial of virtue, the possibility of reform, and the uneasy relation between secular and spiritual meanings, exploit these thematic interests as a test of the reader's understanding of and response to what Richardson calls the "State of Probation." By focusing on their diverse expressions of the "State of Probation," expressions only partly determined by their respective uses of tragic and comic forms, I think we can see that *Clarissa* un-flinchingly represents secular life as a condition of indeterminacy, whereas *Amelia*, even in light of such indeterminacy, yearns for a solution to this condition. Moreover, like Defoe in *Robinson Crusoe* and *Moll Flanders*, Fielding eventually saves his principal characters as well as the reader; but Richardson's view of human nature is such that the majority of his principal characters, and by implication a good many of his readers, are left stranded with their own limited understanding and expectations. Unlike Fielding, Richardson deliberately widens the gap between spiritual and secular meanings, and this may be why he warned that "there are more Lovelaces in the World, than the World imagines."[2]

One way to establish the basically different effects of *Clarissa* and *Amelia* is to consider, first, Richardson's understanding of his tragic novel and its relation to human nature. In his correspondence Richardson writes, "A Writer who follows Nature and pretends to keep the Christian System in his Eye, cannot make a Heaven in this World for his Favourites; or represent this Life otherwise than as a State of Probation. Clarissa I once more averr could not be rewarded in this World" (*SL*, p. 108). In *Hints of Prefaces for Clarissa*, Richardson again insists that "this Life she [Clarissa] looks upon as a Life of Probation only," and in the "Postscript" to *Clarissa* he contrasts—really drives a wedge between—the expectation of poetic justice and his own sense of the state of probation: "And after all, what is the *poetical justice* so much contended for by some, as the generality of writers have managed it, but another sort of dispensation than that which God, by Revelation, teaches us, He has thought fit to exercise mankind; whom placing here only in a state of probation, he hath so intermingled good and evil, as to necessitate us to look forward for a more equal dispensation of both." [3]

Richardson's distinction between religious and literary dispensations is particularly revealing because, while both *Clarissa* and *Amelia* deal with the intermingling of good and evil, Fielding finally implies that good and evil can be sorted out, whereas Richardson believes that the state of probation, which is the state of human nature, involves not only defective knowledge but continued uncertainty. Like Richardson, Johannes Stinstra, who is one of Richardson's most perceptive readers, similarly attacks the expectation of poetic justice because, as he argues, "The human intellect is not equal to the dangers to which we are subject in this life. It is not extensive enough, not intelligent enough, not penetrating enough to know accurately everything that threatens us with harm, and therefore to avoid carefully such dangers." [4]

Now I certainly do not wish to set up Fielding as a straw man; the design of *Amelia* forcefully enacts the very defects of the human intellect that Stinstra and Richardson describe. But beneath Fielding's awareness of human limitations there continues to exist an underlying assurance of providential design which is partly determined by the comic form of *Amelia* and partly a reflection of Fielding's beliefs and temperament. This sense of assurance, in spite of the problematical workings of *Amelia*, is best seen through the character of Dr. Harrison, who not only represents but speaks for the narrative process of *Amelia*. Although Harrison is by no means represented as infallible, he is demonstrably the moral and religious model of the novel, and in this respect he serves Booth and Amelia in the same way that Mrs. Norton, especially, provides religious counsel to Clarissa. On the other hand, Harrison is very much a part of the world, and thus more tolerant of human limitations than either Mrs. Norton or Clarissa. In what may be a statement of the dominant view of human nature in *Amelia*, Harrison chides Amelia when she says "I begin to grow entirely sick of it [the world] . . . for sure all mankind almost are villains in their hearts." Dr. Harrison responds:

Do not make a conclusion so much to the dishonour of the great Creator. The nature of man is far from being in itself evil: it abounds with benevolence, charity, and pity, coveting praise and honour, and shunning shame and disgrace. Bad education, bad habits, and bad customs, debauch our nature, and drive it headlong as it were into vice. The governors of the world, and I am afraid the priesthood, are answerable for the badness of it. Instead of discouraging wickedness to the utmost of their power, both are apt to connive at it.[5]

What Harrison says, and what the whole of *Amelia* continually displays, is that the most dangerous human defects derive from the influence of corrupt social institutions on individual conduct. This is not to say that individuals are without their limitations; obviously every character, including Dr. Harrison and Amelia, makes mistaken judgments, but the moral emphasis of *Amelia*, unlike that of *Clarissa*, is on what Harrison calls bad education, bad habits, and bad customs. Correspondingly, Fielding devotes his most heated comments not to Booth's doctrine of ruling passions—which represents, by the way, a limited understanding of Mandeville—nor to Amelia's naïve estimate of human intentions. Rather Fielding's most acerbic, not to say brutal, observations are reserved for the likes of Mrs. Ellison, Colonel and Mrs. James, the noble lord, Murphy, Trent, Amelia's sister Betty, and other lesser characters who represent such distorted social institutions as the law (not justice), the concept of a gentleman (that is, a rake), honor (hypocrisy), and "modern" marriage—that is pimping for your wife (Trent) or for your husband (Mrs. James). These characters, who represent corrupt social institutions, continually prey on the likes of Amelia and Booth, and their actions, unlike those of Amelia and Booth, are morally culpable because they are consistently premeditated.

Unlike Richardson, then, Fielding emphasizes social institutions as the prevalent threat against a human nature which, in Harrison's words, "abounds with benevolence, charity, and pity," and thus *Amelia*, despite its relatively problematical representation of human life, continues to focus on basically external threats which are, by implication, amenable to external solutions. That is, if bad education, habits, and customs "debauch our nature," it logically—if not in reality—fol-

lows that the correction, or at least detection, of these essentially social
evils will restore human nature to its expected benevolence. Moreover,
this is why Fielding, unlike Richardson, can subscribe to a doctrine of
poetic justice sanctioned by his strong conviction in providential interventions in human affairs. In Richardson's view, however, such providential entrances represent "sudden conversions" which are contrary to
his understanding of human nature, at least as it applies to the problematical design of *Clarissa*. Thus Richardson simply could not or would
not imagine a reformed Lovelace, though he was willing to portray a
reformed Squire B in *Pamela*.

  Since both *Amelia* and *Clarissa* organize their central actions around
the trial of virtue,[6] and since both heroines are represented as fundamentally innocent characters, it may be revealing to compare Fielding's
and Richardson's diverse views of what constitutes innocence and to
examine their use of the trial of virtue as a reflection of their understanding of human nature. Fielding is quite explicit, though seemingly
inconsistent, about this matter in two passages where he openly addresses his readers on the relation of innocence to a corrupt world. In
the first passage Fielding observes: "Hence, my worthy reader, console
thyself, that however few of the other good things of life are thy lot,
the best of all things, which is innocence, is always within thy power;
and though Fortune may make thee often unhappy, she can never make
thee completely and irreparably miserable without thy own consent"
(2:178).

  On the face of it, this passage does not square with Fielding's or
Dr. Harrison's emphasis on social institutions as the root cause of evil.
We are told that innocence is within our "power" and that the loss of
innocence and the misery that attends it involves our "own consent."
The emphasis here seems to fall on individual, rather than social,
responsibility, but the key terms are "power" and "consent." Amelia,
for example, is innocent, but she does not consciously control that
innocence as a power, so much as Fielding allows her mere presence
to exert it. Moreover, when her innocence is threatened by Colonel
James or the noble lord, it is not because she has consented in the
sense that she is a voluntary participant in evil, but only in the sense that
she has unwittingly cooperated with, though finally not participated in,
a corrupt action initiated by someone else. This we can see in the noble
lord's desire to have Amelia attend the masquerade at Ranelagh, or in
Colonel James's offer to have her live with Colonel and Mrs. James

while Booth is away. Similarly, Booth and Mrs. Bennet are initially duped by, respectively, Miss Matthews and the noble lord, but their "consent" involves not only unwitting cooperation but, eventually, knowing participation.

What I am trying to get at in regard to the first passage on innocence has been nicely distinguished by J. Paul Hunter when he says: "Booth and Amelia hold different attitudes toward temptation, he continually placing himself in harm's way and she doing her level best to avoid unnecessary trial." [7] Amelia's innocence is spared not because it is strictly within her power, but because Fielding, through other characters such as Mrs. Bennet, saves her from a trial; this is not, of course, Richardson's way of trying virtue.

The second quotation on innocence is no less interesting and perplexing, especially as it implies the moral culpability of Fielding's readers.

I must inform, therefore, all such readers, that it is not, because innocence is more blind than guilt, that the former often overlooks and tumbles into the pit, which the latter foresees and avoids. The truth is, that it is almost impossible guilt should miss the discovering of all the snares in its way; as it is constantly prying closely into every corner, in order to lay snares for others. Whereas innocence, having no such purpose, walks fearlessly and carelessly through life; and is consequently liable to tread on the gins, which cunning has laid to entrap it. To speak plainly, and without allegory or figure, it is not want of sense, but want of suspicion, by which innocence is often betrayed. . . . In a word, many an innocent person hath owed his ruin to this circumstance alone, that the degree of villainy was such as must have exceeded the faith of every man who was not himself a villain. (2:213)

The passage seems to imply that only on the basis of prior guilt can a character or reader anticipate corrupt motives and actions. Fielding distinguishes between "want of sense" and "want of suspicion," concluding that it is through "want of suspicion" that "innocence is often betrayed." The dilemma is that "suspicion" can be acquired only through the *loss* of innocence, in which case the necessary knowledge to avoid the machinations of a corrupt world is incompatible with innocence. That is, Amelia must be protected by others who *are* suspicious, for her innocence, though desirable, is inadequate in a corrupt world. We must fall to rise, as it were, and while this is very much a part of Richardson's design in *Clarissa*, one wonders whether Fielding realized that this idea or implication tends to undermine the value of Amelia's untested virtue.

Furthermore, it is this very tension between upholding Amelia's value and protecting her innocence, and yet steadily implying that such a value cannot cope with the bad education, customs, and habits of the world, that makes *Amelia*—perhaps inadvertently—the problematical novel that it is. Perhaps this is why critics often note an unresolved tension in the novel. Eric Rothstein remarks on the "general instability of the world of *Amelia*," and he further argues that "the narrator of *Amelia* has retreated, and our attempts to deal with experience put us on the same level with the characters, who fumble blindly." C. J. Rawson comments that "*Amelia* is special among Fielding's novels precisely in that it records irresistible factualities which cannot be mastered by displays of authorial understanding," and, possibly echoing Rawson, J. Paul Hunter suggests that "the radically different tone of *Amelia* seems to me to involve a diminished vision of rhetorical possibility." Such a diminished vision, Hunter later observes, implies "a radical shift in Fielding's view of human nature—from a sense of superficial perversity that goodness could outwit to an overwhelming sense of bad nature prevailing," and this may be what Andrew Wright is referring to when he says, "*Amelia* is the work of a Christian fatalist who was losing his faith in art."[8] All these comments certainly imply that the narrative process, as opposed to the ostensible intent, of *Amelia* was closer to Richardson's understanding of human nature than Fielding was prepared consciously to admit.

On the other hand, Richardson is both explicit and consistent in his view of what constitutes innocence and the trial of virtue. In his correspondence Richardson tells Miss Frances Grainger that "Clarissa was not perfect, but Clarissa could accuse herself in instances where she thought she ought not to be acquitted," and he then goes on to declare: "Calamity is the *test* of virtue, and often the *parent* of it, in minds that prosperity would ruin. What is meant, think you, Madam, by the whole Christian doctrine of the Cross? Ask the people who frequent Vauxhall and Ranelagh if they found themselves fiddled and danced and merry into virtue? What meant the Royal Prophet when he said that it was good for him to be afflicted?" (*SL*, p. 151). In addition, Richardson clearly anticipated that the trial of Clarissa's virtue and her attendant fall would also be a trial of the reader's understanding of the relation between calamity and the exercise of virtue. That is, by writing the novel in such a way that the reader fully participates in Clarissa's trial, Richardson tests the strength of the reader's, as well as the characters', virtue.

This test takes different forms, as we can see in *Hints of Prefaces for Clarissa*, where Richardson distinguishes between "the present light Taste of an Age immersed in Diversions, that engage the Eye and the Ear only, and not the understanding," as opposed to the aims of *Clarissa* which are "to investigate the great Doctrines of Christianity, and to teach the Reader how to die, as well as how to live" (*PHP*, p. 5). Further evidence of how Richardson designed *Clarissa* as a test of the reader may be seen in the laconic remarks that "those who blame Clarissa for Over-niceness, would most probably have been easy prey to a Lovelace," and "many Persons [are] readier to find fault with a supposed perfect Character, than try to imitate it: To bring it down to their Level, rather than rise to it" (*PHP*, p. 5). This echoes Richardson's bitter retort when he rejects the idea of Clarissa marrying a "reformed" Lovelace after the rape: "And is a Clarissa to be reduced to bear so *common* a Lot?" (*SL*, p. 124). But perhaps the most revealing insight into Richardson's estimate of his reader is contained in the observation: "Clarissa an Example *to* the Reader: The Example not to be taken *from* the Reader" (*PHP*, p. 5).

If we apply some of these observations to the characters in the novel, we can see why Richardson finally mistrusts many of his characters and readers, who seem more allured by the eye and ear than enlightened by the novel's understanding. Elizabeth Brophy has shrewdly noted that "each confidant acts as a surrogate for the reader," and it is fascinating to see how Richardson measures and tests the reader's understanding in the same way that the spectrum of characters responds to Clarissa's ordeal.[9] For example, Anna Howe—not Clarissa—is the first to realize the depth and probable intent of Lovelace's superficially pleasing actions. Early on she warns Clarissa:

But, O my friend, depend upon it, you are in danger. . . . Your native generosity and greatness of mind endanger you: All your friends, by fighting *against* him with impolitic violence, fight *for* him. And Lovelace, my life for yours, notwithstanding all his veneration and assiduities, has seen further than that veneration and those assiduities (so well calculated to your meridian) will let him own he has seen—Has seen, in short, that his work is doing for him more effectually than he could do it for himself. . . . In short, my dear, it is my opinion, and that from the easiness of his heart and behaviour, that he has seen

more than *I* have seen; more than you think *could* be seen;—more than I
believe you *yourself* know, or else you would have let me know it.[10]

Not only is Anna right, but paradoxically, the strength of her perception is determined in large part by her too easy identification with Lovelace's motives, even though she cannot fathom the full extent of his
contrivance. Richardson enables Anna to detect Lovelace because,
throughout *Clarissa*, we get numerous versions—positive and negative
—of "It takes one to know one," and this applies to the reader's
response as well. Anna puts it more politely when she tells Clarissa:
"I am fitter for *this* world than you: You for the *next* than me;—that's
the difference" (1:63).

    Clearly Anna Howe is not a "rake," but Richardson does call her
"a true modern wit, who thinks it not necessary, when it carries the
keenest edge, to retain discretion in its service" (*SL*, p. 166). Furthermore, we do know that Anna is, to Clarissa's eventual dismay, far more
attracted to Lovelace than to Hickman, who is a man of virtue.[11] Anna
is a contriver, especially with her mother, and her cleverness, which is
based on a knowledge Clarissa initially lacks, enables her to anticipate
Lovelace's motives, if not the precise design of his actions. Moreover,
the knowledge Anna possesses is a precise corollary to what Fielding
calls "suspicion."

    Throughout *Clarissa* Richardson distinguishes between "sense"
and "suspicion," except his terms are "theory" and "practice" (or
"experience"). Anna Howe reminds Clarissa of one of Mrs. Norton's
observations, "'that to excel in theory, and to excel in practice, generally required different talents; which did not always meet in the same
person'" (2:10), but the value of these differing "talents" is perhaps
more problematical than it appears. For one thing, the person with
maximum "experience" is Lovelace, and it is he more than anyone else
who tosses around this distinction. Referring to Clarissa and Anna
Howe, he tells Belford: "Silly little rogues! to walk out into by-paths
on the strength of their own judgments!—When nothing but *experience* can enable them to disappoint us, and teach them grandmother-
wisdom!" (3:199). Later Lovelace says of Clarissa, "This dear Lady is
prodigiously learned in *Theories*. But as to *Practics*, as to *Experi-
mentals*, must be, as you know from her tender years, a mere novice"
(3:353); and he repeats this formulation when he asks: "Yet, what can
be expected of an angel under Twenty?—She has a world of knowl-

edge; knowledge *speculative*, as I may say; but not *Experience!* How should she?—Knowledge by theory only is a vague uncertain light: A Will o' the Wisp, which as often misleads the doubting mind, as puts it right" (5:122).

Because Richardson believes calamity is the test of virtue, and because he believes that this life is a state of probation, he does not, like Fielding, protect his heroine from "experience." Rather he submits her to experience—dramatically represented by the rape—in order finally to celebrate her virtue. The rape, if you will, stands for the way of the world, just as Lovelace fancies himself the man of experience, but Clarissa's response to the rape demonstrates the strength of her virtue in the face of an experience more brutal than anything in *Amelia*. Just as important, Richardson through Clarissa's trial submits the reader to a similar test regarding theoretical and practical knowledge, for these two terms operate in much the same way as what I have called observation and experience.

One way that Richardson establishes this test, and it is a way that distinguishes Richardson's narrative process from Fielding's, may be seen by comparing two critical observations on the problematical workings of *Amelia* and *Clarissa*. Robert Alter writes: "The strategies of *Amelia* . . . generally lead us toward a closer involvement in the moral predicaments of the novel, and, to a lesser degree, in the lives of the characters." In a somewhat similar manner, Mark Kinkead-Weekes says of *Clarissa* that "our first experience is one of moral evaluation, of continuous analysis, of living in a mind that submits every detail of action and thought to intensive and scrupulous examination." [12] Taken in the abstract, such comments might suggest that *Amelia* and *Clarissa* submit the reader to similar interpretive challenges, and to a certain extent this is true. In both novels the reader, like the principal characters, is actively engaged in moral predicaments, but the predicaments of *Clarissa* are a good deal more demanding because they are far more indeterminate.

For example, Amelia tries to convert Booth from his atheistic principle of self-love by first encouraging him to "converse with Dr. Harrison on this subject; for I am sure he would convince you, though I can't, that there are really such things as religion and virtue" (3:127). Her appeal is wholly to Harrison's reason and powers of persuasion because her virtue is finally inactive. When Booth is converted to Christianity by reading Dr. Barrow's sermons—Fielding's *deus ex machina*

—Fielding sets up the following conversation between Booth and Harrison in such a way that it is calculated to affect the reader, ostensibly solving one of the novel's moral predicaments. Booth says:

"I have not a doubt (for I own I have had such) which remains now unsatisfied.—If ever an angel might be thought to guide the pen of a writer, surely the pen of that great and good man had such an assistant." The doctor readily concurred in the praises of Dr. Barrow, and added—"You say you have had your doubts, young gentleman; indeed, I did not know that—And pray, what were your doubts?" "Whatever they were, sir," said Booth, "they are now satisfied, as I believe those of every impartial and sensible reader will be, if he will, with due attention, read over these excellent sermons." (3:211)

Such a passage is consistent with Fielding's benevolent and rational expectations concerning human nature, but it is also fair to say that the reader is left wholly in the position of an outside observer. We do not know, specifically, what in Barrow's sermons converted Booth, nor do we, any more than Harrison, know the precise nature of Booth's doubts, unless we accept the casual formula of self-love. We are simply told that Booth is "satisfied," though clearly a number of critics are not, and the reader is explicitly told that he will achieve a similar satisfaction if he reads over "these excellent sermons." The resolution of this moral predicament, in other words, is entirely exterior, and unlike Richardson, who subjects the reader to far more demanding tests, Fielding ends up doing most of the work for the reader because he, like Barrow, has a much stronger assurance of providential intervention into the ways of a corrupt world.

If we take one phrase from the quoted passage—"due attention"— we can see how Richardson uses his moral predicaments to involve the reader in sterner, and correspondingly less determinate, tests. Johannes Stinstra construes attention as one of the key processes through which Richardson tests his readers.[13] Stinstra reduces "everything into one requirement which this work may justly demand of all its readers. . . . an exact attention and regard concerning everything we meet in it" (*Stinstra*, p. 144), and he goes on to display what such a reading will attend to:

Through the personalities of the characters we perceive their different moral conditions, according to which their deliberations, conversations, undertakings, and actions are so very different from each other just as the differences in countenance, features, shape, and bearing are clearly discernible among thousands of people, each from all the others. These are not composed of morally good or bad qualities only but are also mingled with different natural attributes, whether these be innate or acquired passively through education, conversation, and habit. . . . we should trace and deliberate the aims of the author with all our attention: what he wants to represent and show regarding human behavior and way of acting by his work in general and in its particular parts and what he wants to teach and point out to us in these revelations regarding our morals and actions. These moral aims of the writer must be clearly distinguished from the aims of the characters whom he introduces through speaking or writing. . . . [moreover] something else is required of us to comprehend fully the moral aim of the author. . . . this is the spiritual sense of the work, as the divines put it, and without it, all the rest is but dead words. (*Stinstra*, pp. 151, 155, 156)

Such an attentive reading imposes tremendous hardships on the reader because it unrelentingly exercises and measures the strength of our virtue. That is, not only are the moral predicaments of *Clarissa* fully internalized by the various characters, but they require a corresponding assimilation by the reader.

This we can see quite clearly in two passages that display the problematic workings of the novel. In the first passage Clarissa dramatizes her predicament in response to Anna Howe's well-meaning but uncertain advice, and her response further distinguishes between Anna's external observation and Clarissa's extraordinary entanglement:

Had you, my dear, been witness to my different emotions, as I read your Letter, when, in one place, you advise me of my danger, if I am carried to my Uncle's; in another, when you own you could not bear what I bear, and would do anything rather than marry the man you hate; yet, in another, represent to me my reputation suffering in the world's eye; and the necessity I should be under to justify my conduct, at the expence of my friends, were I to take a rash step; in another, insinuate the *dishonest* figure I should be forced to make, in so compelled a Matrimony; endeavouring to cajole, fawn upon, and play the hypocrite with a man to whom I have an aversion; who would have reason to *believe* me an hypocrite, as well from my former avowals, as from the sense he *must* have (if common sense he has) of his own demerits:—The necessity you think there would be for me, the more averse I really was, to seem the fonder of him: A fondness (were I capable of such dissimulation) that would be imputable to disgraceful motives; as it would be too visible, that Love, either of person or mind, could be neither of them—Then his undoubted, his even constitutional narrowness; His too probable jealousy, and unforgivingness, bearing in mind my declared aversion and the unfeigned despights I took all opportunities to do him, in order to discourage his address: A preference avowed against him from the *same* motive: with the pride he professes to take in curbing and sinking the spirits of a woman he had acquired a right to tyrannize over:—Had you, I say, been witness of my different emotions as I read; now leaning this way, now that; now perplexed; now apprehensive; now angry at one, then at another; now resolving; now doubting;—you would have seen the power you have over me; and would have had reason to believe, that, had you given your advice in any determined or positive manner, I had been ready to have been concluded by it. (2:75–76)

Any reader who attends to this sentence has to participate in its meaning in order to assimilate and thereby reexperience the trial that Clarissa undergoes. Although the sentence begins and rewinds to the subjunctive "Had you," by the time the reader has gone through the sentence it is a living and present experience. Moreover, because the questions Clarissa faces and poses are neither easily formulated nor easily resolved, this sentence, like the novel, produces further and deeper entanglements. The very length of this unusual sentence, like the length of the novel, mirrors and duplicates the complication and indeterminacy of what Richardson calls the state of probation. In fact, the only people who continually operate in a distinctly "positive manner" are the other members of the Harlowe family, who are a grotesque parody of determination; ironically, not even Lovelace nor Sinclair, in their most calculating and menacing moments, lack doubt.

Indeed, Clarissa's complicated sentence serves as a kind of paradigm of the reader's experience, for it invites reasoning at the same time that it frustrates it, which is to say the reader, like Clarissa, now leans this way, now that; is now perplexed, now apprehensive; now resolves, now doubts. It is no wonder that Kinkead-Weekes, commenting on the novel's indeterminacy, has argued that "the 'meanings' which emerge from this way of writing are bound to be more tentative and more complicated than in other kinds of fiction, since many more tensions and problems arise than the author anticipated, or can immediately clarify." However, if we draw the further conclusion, as Eaves and Kimpel do, that "the 'meaning' of *Clarissa* is the experience which the reader has while he reads the book," then we run the risk of placing too much emphasis on the adequacy of the secular self—the characters' as well as the reader's—without realizing that this self and its capacity to reason promote the very illusions of control that the novel continually undermines.[14]

Anna Howe, for example, proposes a formula for Clarissa's trial of virtue that is finally inadequate to the novel's and Clarissa's ordeal. In the first letter of the novel Anna tells Clarissa, "Yet it must be allowed, that your present trial is but proportioned to your prudence" (1:3); and after the rape Anna again insists that Lovelace's "attempts were but proportioned to your resistance and vigilance" (6:199). But the truth is—and this is why *Clarissa* is a tragic novel—that the moral predicaments of the novel are disproportionate to Clarissa's or anyone else's virtue, for there is no rational way that Clarissa or, by implication, the reader could successfully anticipate, not to say resist, Lovelace's premeditated violence. In fact, it is Belford who sees that "the trial is not a fair trial" (3:265); he tells Lovelace:

Considering the depth of thy plots and contrivances: Considering the opportunities which I see thou must have with her, in spite of her own heart; all her Relations follies acting in concert, though unknown to themselves, with thy wicked scheming head: Considering how destitute of protection she is: Considering the house [Sinclair's] she is to be in, where she will be surrounded with thy implements; *specious*, *well-bred*, and *genteel* creatures, not easily to be detected when they are disposed to preserve appearances, especially by a young, unexperienced Lady wholly unacquainted with the town: Considering all these things, I say, what glory, what cause of triumph, wilt thou have, if she should be overcome? . . . It would be a miracle if she stood such an attempter, such attempts, and such snares, as I see will be laid for her. (3:265–66)

As Belford's quotation implies, there is simply too much for Clarissa or the reader to "consider"—not to say control—and thus our expectations of rational control are correspondingly undermined. A considerable part of the novel's "calamity" depends on Richardson's ability to overload the processes of reasoning, ensnaring both the characters and the reader in their own rational expectations; this is what Clarissa is getting at when she distinguishes between her own "wilderness of doubt and error" and the basically external and limited view of "the event-judging world" (4:38–39). The "event-judging world," as I understand it, basically judges the fact of an action, rather than the motives behind it; moreover, such judgments presume the self-sufficiency of reason and what I have called the adequacy of self. But this is precisely the process which is Clarissa's initial weakness, and which continues to be the weakness of any readings that assume the adequacy of self and the proportionate strength of individual reason and reform. Clarissa condemns herself for "too much indeed relying upon her own strength," but she speaks for all the characters, and a good many readers, when she also chastises herself for having "thought I could *proceed*, or *stop*, as I pleased" (2:361).

In short, too much attention has been focused on Clarissa's self or individuality when this is exactly what she perceives to be her central and fatal weakness. The novel, for instance, certainly invites psychological interpretations, but one wonders whether this kind of reading doesn't finally entrap itself in the very presumption that Clarissa eventually escapes. Diverse critics have argued that "the pervasiveness of fantasy in the creation of character is . . . Richardson's preeminent contribution to the novel," that both Lovelace and Clarissa "acknowledge, in quite different ways, the freedom of the will, the sovereignty of self," and that "self-suffering and self-creation is the general message of the novel, and Richardson spoke to a world ready for that message."[15] Such insistent secular readings hardly jibe with Mrs. Norton's counsel to Clarissa: "If you are to be punished all your days here, for example-sake, in a case of such importance, for your one false step, be pleased to consider, That this Life is but a State of Probation; and if you have your Purification in it, you will be the more happy. Nor doubt I, that you will have the higher Reward *hereafter* for submitting to the Will of Providence *here*, with Patience and Resignation" (6:128–29).

Mrs. Norton's understanding certainly conforms with Richardson's declared views on the state of probation, and despite Ian Watt's puzzling comment about Richardson's "shallow notion of religion,"[16] I think it is evident that the novel leaves such secular readings as his entirely at the level of indeterminacy, just as Clarissa abandons her initial preoccupation with self for the more assured, though less measurable, future rewards of piety. The "Patience and Resignation" to which Mrs. Norton refers require an abandonment of self, and it is exactly this abandonment of self that Clarissa asserts in one of her posthumous letters:

I was too apt to value myself upon the love and favour of every one: The merit of the good I delighted to do, and of the inclinations which were given me, and which I could not *help* having, I was, perhaps, too ready to attribute to myself. . . . Temptations were accordingly sent. I shrunk in the day of tryal. My discretion, which had been so cried up, was found wanting when it came to be weighed in an equal balance. I was betrayed, fell, and became the byword of my companions, and a disgrace to my family, which had prided itself in me perhaps too much. But as my fault was not that of a culpable will, when my pride was sufficiently mortified, I was not suffered (altho' surrounded by dangers, and entangled in snares) to be totally lost: But purified by sufferings, I was fitted for the change I have NOW, at the time you will receive This, so newly, and, as I humbly hope, so happily, experienced. (8:31)

Quite appropriately John Preston writes that "the novel ends by depicting the kind of response it desires," but evidently it is not the kind of experience desired by some readers, nor understood by a majority of the characters.[17]

Interestingly, when Clarissa declares herself to be "so newly, and . . . so happily, experienced," she has in fact collapsed the novel's earlier distinction (and Lovelace's obsession) between theory and practice or experience; for this distinction, we can now see, is inadequate because it is unable, finally, either to include or explain the kind of "experience" Clarissa has acquired. Clarissa is not using the term "experience" to refer to secular life or secular understanding, and this point is underscored by the fact that it appears in a posthumous letter when she must be understood as "speaking from the dead" (8:138). The "NOW" that she mentions, moreover, does not refer to the secular present time that dominates the novel, but rather to her presence in another spiritual world which transcends the state of probation. This is the spiritual sense of the work, and without it, as Stinstra puts it, "all the rest is but dead words."

Furthermore, Richardson concludes the novel with an apt reading paradigm that tests the reader's and characters' ability to differentiate between the spiritual sense and the "dead words" of exclusively secular readings. Just as Clarissa rejects the temporal solutions to her ordeal—she neither wishes to prosecute Lovelace in court, nor does she seek the vengeance that Morden finally inflicts on Lovelace—so the "meaning" of Clarissa's trial ultimately exceeds the grasp of a variety of characters who are themselves too immersed in their own preoccupations with self and rational understanding. This is made especially clear in Clarissa's cryptic letter to Lovelace in which she speaks on a wholly spiritual level:

I have good news to tell you. I am setting out with all diligence for my Father's House. I am bid to hope that he will receive his poor penitent with a goodness peculiar to himself; for I am overjoyed with the assurance of a thorough Reconciliation, thro' the interposition of a dear blessed friend, whom I always loved and honoured. . . . So, pray, Sir, don't disturb or interrupt me—I beseech you don't. You may possibly in time see me at my Father's; at least, if it be not your own fault. (7:189–90)

The responses of a variety of characters to this letter serves to indicate how Richardson, unlike Fielding, refuses to accommodate Clarissa's trial to the limited understanding and expectations of secular life. The reforming Belford reads the letter and confesses to Clarissa: "Indeed, Madam, I can find nothing but that you are going down to Harlowe-Place to be reconciled to your Father and other Friends" (7:272). And after Clarissa explains its religious meaning, he chides himself and Lovelace for their "own Stupidity, to be thus taken in" (7:273) by their secular preoccupation with a resolution, or happy ending, in this world. In the same way Lovelace, Morden, and Lord M. ponder Clarissa's letter, each trying to enforce a meaning on it that satisfies his expectations but in fact reveals his own conspicuous limitations. Lovelace, for instance, wants to believe that Morden is Clarissa's "*dear blessed friend*" (7:301), and Morden is only too happy to comply with this reading, though he still worries that "I know not what to make of it" (7:302). Lord M. wants to think, though it is phrased as a question, that "there is something very favourable to my Nephew in this Letter—Something that looks as if the Lady would comply at last?" (7:302). But Lovelace finally condemns the letter as deceit, arguing that "she sat down to write this letter with a design to mislead and deceive. And if she be capable of That, at such a crisis, she has as much need of *Heaven's* forgiveness, as I have of *hers*" (7:329).

Such confusion about the meaning of Clarissa's letter is a powerful and illuminating way of summarizing and testing not only the characters', but the reader's, distance from God and immersion in this world. Fielding can resolve, if not clarify, the moral predicaments of *Amelia* with Dr. Harrison's upbeat assertion to Booth that "your sufferings are all at an end; and Providence hath done you the justice at last, which it will one day or other render to all men" (3:226). But in *Clarissa* Richardson's view of the state of probation is such as not to allow for happy endings, nor for the reformation of rakes, because "he always thought, that *sudden conversions*, such especially, as were left to the candour of the Reader to *suppose* and *make out*, had neither *Art*, nor *Nature*, nor even *Probability*, in them; and that they were moreover of very *bad* example" (*PHP*, p. 349). Indeed, it is this mistaken expectation of "sudden conversions" that dominates the various characters' interpretations of Clarissa's letter, for they understand, because they want to believe, that Clarissa's "reconciliation" will be with this world, just as so many of Richardson's contemporaries desired a happy ending.

Alan McKillop reports that among Richardson's contemporaries Fielding was one of those who "wrote a letter to Richardson urging a happy ending."[18] But such a happy ending, based on the desired reform of Lovelace, represents an accommodation to the world that would undermine Richardson's sense of secular existence as a state of probation. Part of the reason that Clarissa must die is that Richardson wished to frustrate the reader's worldly expectations. For example, he writes in his correspondence: "I had further intended to make her [Clarissa] so faultless, that a Reader should find no way to account for the Calamities she met with, and to justify Moral Equity but by looking up to a future Reward" (*SL*, p. 73). Richardson further insists on Clarissa's "triumphant Death" over "the World" (*SL*, p. 87), and he addresses the following acrimonious response to Lady Bradshaigh who, like Fielding, hoped for a happy ending: "I am sorry that it was supposed that I had no other end in the Publication of so large a Piece, the Opening of which had extended to four close printed Volumes, but the trite one of perfecting a private Happiness, by the Reformation of a Libertine, who sinning against the Light of Knowledge, and against the most awaking Calls & Convictions, was too determined a Libertine to be reformed, at least till he arrived at the Age of Incapacity" (*SL*, p. 103).[19]

What finally differentiates the problematical effects of *Amelia* and *Clarissa* is that they address and challenge the "incapacity" of their readers in widely different ways. Both novels share an intense pre-occupation with the trial of virtue, the possibility of reform, and the relationship between secular and spiritual orders of experience. Yet Fielding can adopt what Richardson calls "sudden conversions" because his view of human nature presumes the possibility of reform through providential interventions in the secular world. Thus he can finally reinforce the reader's desire for solutions—rational and religious —to the moral predicaments of this world, though Fielding is at the same time distrustful of the characters' and reader's unassisted reliance on reason. To this extent, I certainly agree with Eric Rothstein's statement that "like the conclusion of *Clarissa* or of *Rasselas*, though not so thoroughly, the end of *Amelia* admits the vanity of human wishes in a tawdry and dangerous world."[20]

But where Fielding admits the vanity of human wishes only to clarify them, Richardson no less appropriately both admits them and deepens them, for he refuses to extricate his readers from moral predicaments. Clarissa alone escapes the clutches of this world, just as she escapes the reader's desire for containment, and the novel thereby frustrates, in a way that *Amelia* does not, the reader's desire for secular reconciliation. This continued frustration of the reader is a necessary corollary to Richardson's dramatization of the problematical nature of human existence. The state of probation from which the reader, unlike Clarissa, is not removed continues as a condition of indeterminacy; and though the dying Lovelace may remorsefully declare, "LET THIS EXPIATE!" (8:277), there is in *Clarissa* no satisfactory expiation in this world.

6
Johnson's Equipoise and the State of Man

As I argued in the last chapter, Richardson and Fielding are both concerned with the religious life of their characters and readers, but these two authors address themselves to the reader's and characters' "State of Probation" in vastly different ways. Fielding wishes to enact the possibility of religious conversion, even in the face of an overwhelmingly defective secular world, but Richardson rejects the possibility of Lovelace's conversion because this would falsify the uncompromising tragic severity of Clarissa's Christian dying to the world. Like Richardson and Fielding, Johnson takes for granted—more than he uses as his focus—the fallen nature of man, but in *The Life of Savage* and *Rasselas* Johnson opts neither for Richardson's Christian rigor nor for Fielding's "sudden conversions." Instead, he attends to the more modest possibility of choosing and acting virtuously in a clearly imperfect world. I do not wish to be understood as saying that Johnson rejects the realm of Christian faith; rather I think it can be shown that he believes the state of religious belief to surpass the affective possibilities of imaginative literature. The fundamental appeal of literature, as Johnson understands it, must be adjusted to the reader's secular existence—to the peculiar blend of human strengths and weaknesses; correspondingly, what Johnson's writings repeatedly evoke is the reader's sense of "virtue not angelical, nor above probability . . . but the highest and purest that humanity can reach."[1]

The implications of what Johnson means by "the highest and purest that humanity can reach" emerge most forcefully in his criticism of *Paradise Lost*. Before I quote this section, the reader should be reminded, first, that it occurs after Johnson commends *Paradise Lost* as "a poem which, considered with respect to

design, may claim the first place, and with respect to performance the
second, among the productions of the human mind";[2] and, second,
that Johnson's criticism arises, paradoxically, from what he takes to be
Milton's imaginative strength: namely, his magnificent sublimity which
has the "peculiar power to astonish" (*Lives*, 1:177).

> The plan of *Paradise Lost* has this inconvenience, that it comprises neither
> human actions nor human manners. The man and woman who act and suffer
> are in a state which no other man or woman can ever know. The reader finds
> no transaction in which he can be engaged, beholds no condition in which he
> can by any effort of imagination place himself; he has, therefore, little natural
> curiosity or sympathy.
>   We all, indeed, feel the effects of Adam's disobedience; we all sin like
> Adam, and like him must all bewail our offences; we have restless and in-
> sidious enemies in the fallen angels, and in the blessed spirits we have guardians
> and friends; in the Redemption of mankind we hope to be included: in the
> description of heaven and hell we are surely interested, as we are all to reside
> hereafter in the regions of horrour or of bliss.
>   But these truths are too important to be new: they have been taught to our
> infancy; they have mingled with our solitary thoughts and familiar conversa-
> tion, and are habitually interwoven with the whole texture of life. Being there-
> fore not new they raise no unaccustomed emotion in the mind: what we knew
> before we cannot learn; what is not unexpected, cannot surprise. . . . Pleasure
> and terrour are indeed the genuine sources of poetry; but poetical pleasure must
> be such as human imagination can at least conceive, and poetical terrour such
> as human strength and fortitude may combat. . . .
>   But original deficience cannot be supplied. The want of human interest is
> always felt. *Paradise Lost* is one of the books which the reader admires and
> lays down, and forgets to take up again. None ever wishes it longer than it is.
> Its perusal is a duty rather than a pleasure. (*Lives*, 1:181–83)

The drift of these paragraphs is clear, consistent, and possibly dis-
turbing. Johnson is saying that the reader can enter into acts of imagination only by virtue of what he has experienced. Acts of imagination
need not correspond to duplicate human experiences, but taking pleasure and terror as the root experiences of poetry, they must be such
that "human imagination can at least conceive" and "human strength
and fortitude may combat." Johnson is arguing that the images of
Paradise Lost, and hence its sentiments (or meaning), reside outside
the power of the reader's imagination, even though the poem is the
product of a human act. Thus Leopold Damrosch has accurately ob-

served that Johnson's treatment of *Paradise Lost* "depends upon the idea that Milton has overreached the bounds of human nature."[3] The reader cannot fully participate in the sentiments of *Paradise Lost* because Adam and Eve "act and suffer in a state which no other man or woman can ever know." For Johnson, the only experience of paradise he can successfully imagine is the experience of paradise *lost;* he cannot experience Adam and Eve's state of innocence. When Johnson writes that the "reader finds no transaction in which he can be engaged" he is referring to the initial experience of trying to read *Paradise Lost*, and saying that the images are such that they do not elicit what, in *Rambler 60*, he calls a "uniformity in the state of man." The state of man, as Johnson understands it, is not a state of innocence. In Johnson's reading, the only experience the reader can fully imagine is the loss of paradise. Because the reader begins in a state of fallen experience where Adam and Eve only end—namely, east of Eden—Adam and Eve cannot exist until the end of the poem within the reader's experiential frame of reference. Thus, in Johnson's view, Adam and Eve—and the sentiments of *Paradise Lost*—remain primarily formulations, rather than experiences, of truths. Or, as he writes of the sentiments: "Being therefore not new they raise no unaccustomed emotion in the mind: what we knew before we cannot learn; what is not unexpected, cannot surprise."

Here we arrive at a crucial point in Johnson's understanding of the relation between literature, religious belief, and human nature. Johnson clearly suggests an inexorable division between the truths of religion and the imaginative appeal of literature. This division assumes that religious truths, such as those in *Paradise Lost*, are beyond the scope of literary invention. This controversial assumption not only appears in *The Life of Milton;* it is also vigorously asserted in both the *Life of Cowley* and the *Life of Waller:*

The whole system of life, while the Theocracy was yet visible, has an appearance so different from all other scenes of human action that the reader of the Sacred Volume habitually considers it as the peculiar mode of existence of a distinct species of mankind, that lived and acted with manners uncommunicable; so that it is difficult even for imagination to place us in the state of them whose story is related, and by consequence their joys and griefs are not easily adopted, nor can the attention be often interested in any thing that befalls them. (*Lives*, 1:51)

Let no pious ear be offended if I advance, in opposition to many authorities, that poetical devotion cannot often please. . . . Contemplative piety, or the intercourse between God and the human soul, cannot be poetical. Man admitted to implore the mercy of his Creator and plead the merits of his Redeemer is already in a higher state than poetry can confer. (*Lives*, 1:291)

On the other hand, the state of experience that poetry, or literature generally, can confer is stated explicitly in *Rambler 60:*

All joy or sorrow for the happiness or calamities of others is produced by an act of the imagination, that realises the event however fictitious, or approximates it however remote, by placing us, for a time, in the condition of him whose fortune we contemplate; so that we feel, while the deception lasts, whatever motions would be excited by the same good or evil happening to ourselves. . . . Those parallel circumstances, and kindred images, to which we readily conform our minds, are, above all other writings, to be found in narratives of the lives of particular persons; and therefore no species of writing seems more worthy of cultivation than biography, since none can be more delightful or more useful, none can more certainly enchain the heart by irresistible interest, or more widely diffuse instruction to every diversity of condition. (*Rambler*, 3:318–19)

The "motions" to which Johnson refers derive from his fundamental premise that "there is such an uniformity in the state of man, considered apart from adventitious and separable decorations and disguises, that there is scarce any possibility of good or ill, but is common to human kind." This premise is the principle by which Johnson links up the particular (an individual life) with the general (humankind). Johnson assumes an underlying uniformity of mankind which is essentially moral and cognitive: "We are all prompted by the same motives, all deceived by the same fallacies, all animated by hope, obstructed by danger, entangled by desire, and seduced by pleasure." This uniformity combines a moral sense with a strong sense of individuation, and by refusing to concentrate on the one to the exclusion of the other Johnson generates an affective appeal that is flexibly adjusted to the reader's strengths and limitations. Moreover, Johnson's writings are not simply designed as acts of the imagination which the reader may intellectually contemplate; rather Johnson continually appeals to the reader's willingness to exert a corresponding act of imagination, wherein he places himself for a time "in the condition of him whose fortune we con-

template," so that the reader can apprehend—which is to say participate in—"whatever motions would be excited by the same good or
evil happening to ourselves." [4]

In other words, Johnson initially assumes his own ability, and subsequently extends the reader's sympathetic capacity, to respond to the
underlying motions of mind of persons whose character, social situation, or human predicaments may at first glance appear to be totally
unlike his own. For example, the *Life of Savage* is certainly, on one
level, a biography of a particular man and his specific circumstances.
But because Johnson assumes that there exists "an uniformity in the
state of man," he eventually strips the particular life of Savage of its
"adventitious and separable decorations and disguises" in order to
make the reader participate in the emotional and intellectual correspondences that exist between Savage's life and his own. [5] In a sense, then,
the biography of Savage becomes the occasion for the reader to com-
pose in an act of imagination a biography of himself. We are asked to
measure ourselves against Savage, just as Johnson evidently realizes
some similarities between himself and Savage. [6] In this way Johnson
transforms Savage's individual life into an analysis of what Clarence
Tracy has called "one of the strangest, most fascinating, and most
revealing specimens of human nature that any biographer ever dealt
with." [7]

One such passage that evokes Johnson's sense of humanity's virtues
and defects occurs when Savage meets the woman whose testimony
led to his imprisonment:

She informed him, that she was in Distress, and, with a Degree of Confidence
not easily attainable, desired him to relieve her. He, instead of insulting her
Misery, and taking Pleasure in the Calamities of one who had brought his Life
into Danger, reproved her gently for her Perjury, and changing the only Guinea
that he had, divided it equally between her and himself.

This is an Action which in some Ages would have made a Saint, and perhaps in others a Hero, and which, without any hyperbolical Encomiums, must
be allowed to be an Instance of uncommon Generosity, an Act of complicated
Virtue; by which he at once relieved the Poor, corrected the Vicious, and for-
gave an Enemy; by which he at once remitted the strongest Provocations, and
exercised the most ardent Charity. (*Savage*, p. 40)

For most readers, I would suspect, this passage comes as a surprise. Skeptical readers, especially, are no doubt tempted to dismiss

the story as being both superficially tendentious and quite possibly apocryphal. Moreover, even if the story is true, it smacks of melodrama: the unjustly imprisoned victim, falsely accused of murder, emerges from prison and by an act of divine coincidence encounters the woman whose perjured testimony—or so it is alleged—has helped to convict him; the victim, in an act of magnificent charity, not only forgives her and gently rebukes her, but gives her money—half of his money—and sends her on her way. And yet I think, though I cannot prove, that Johnson expected such extremes of response—be they sentimental or skeptical—not simply to shock or amaze his readers, but to provoke us into further inquiry about how this "Act of Complicated Virtue" is representative of the "state of man."

One way of examining this passage and its resonances is to consider one of the definitions for the word "complicate" in Johnson's dictionary: "To entangle one with another; to join." To illumine this definition Johnson quotes a passage from Watts: "There are a multitude of human actions, which have so many *complicated* circumstances, aspects, and situations, with regard to time and place, persons and things, that it is impossible for any one to pass a right judgment concerning them, without entering into most of these circumstances." Johnson's choice of the word "complicated" in the *Life of Savage* is altogether appropriate, for it serves as a shorthand term for the very process of reading that Johnson expects of his readers. That is, the only adequate way for us to attempt an assessment of Savage is to enter into—rather than detach ourselves from—the circumstances surrounding his life.

This process of "complicated" reading emerges quite forcefully in the second paragraph of the quoted passage from the *Life of Savage*, which is devoted to Johnson's interpretation of the event and to his anticipation of how the reader may be responding to Savage's act. The apparent aspects of melodrama are introduced, I believe, in anticipation of the reader's potential stock responses. It would not be surprising if many readers thought of Savage's act, in light of the background of perjury and imprisonment, as one verging on the saintly or heroic, but Johnson actually enhances the value of Savage's action, and hence makes it more plausible, by reducing it from apparent heroism to a level more familiar and more accessible to his readers.

The first part of Johnson's sentence reads, "This is an Action which in some Ages would have made a Saint, and perhaps in others a Hero, and which without any hyperbolical Encomiums, must be allowed to be an Instance of uncommon Generosity, an Act of complicated Virtue." The effect of this sentence is to push back notions of saintliness and heroism into a distant past, to associate these notions when introduced into the present with "hyperbolical Encomiums," and yet to maintain with determined authority ("must be allowed") the "uncommon," which is not to say that it could not *become* common, generosity of Savage's action. Through this reported event Johnson anticipates and almost immediately deflates any temptation on the reader's part to react to Savage's life either skeptically or sentimentally. For Johnson the author, and Savage the ostensible subject, this event and the many events of Savage's life are "complicated." Johnson's decision to relate an event like this is evidently calculated to move the reader from a position of detached observation to that of imaginative participation. The relation of this event overturns stock responses by refusing to elevate Savage's action out of a human context, and thus resisting the temptation to "canonize" him on the basis of a single action. Yet the event complicates the reader's psychological and moral understanding because it reminds him, whether he has or has not suffered hardships similar to Savage's, that acts of "complicated Virtue," even under the most adverse circumstances, are well within human capabilities, humanly desirable, and indispensable to our understanding of Savage.

I have tried to emphasize, through the example of one recorded event in the *Life of Savage*, how the reader is required to participate within the process of Johnson's narrative because I am convinced that one of Johnson's great strengths is his sensitivity to human cognition and psychology—to "what is common to human kind"—not by virtue of some elaborate theoretical framework which he has rationally formulated, but by virtue of his compassionate understanding of what it means to be a human being. While I am not sure whether Johnson, as Donald Greene has suggested, "may well be considered the originator of modern psychological biography," I certainly do agree with Greene that Johnson has a masterful practical grasp of human psychology.[8] A failure to respond to the psychological processes in the *Life* has led one critic to argue that the work "is conducted so that it becomes a virtual eighteenth-century type-comedy of the dynamics of hopes and 'schemes.'"[9] Such an abstract approach presumes the reader's detached sense of superiority to Savage's experiences, while Johnson continually undercuts such expectations. This very tendency or temptation toward abstract observation, as Johnson shows, is one of the fundamental weaknesses of Savage's character, and I should think that the following passage might well serve as a warning to readers and critics alike about the danger of imposing abstract labels on *The Life of Savage:* "But these Reflections, though they readily occurred to him in the first and last Parts of his Life, were, I am afraid, for a long Time forgotten; at least they were, like many other maxims, treasured up in his Mind, rather for Shew than Use" (*Savage*, p. 67). One danger of abstractions, in other words, is that the reader may end up reading the *Life* in the same way that Savage treasured up maxims—"rather for Shew than Use." This would occur if the reader concentrated exclusively on the purely formal qualities of the biography, and ignored the imaginative processes enacted by the biography which give it its "symbolic force." [10]

Another way of seeing how Johnson transforms a potentially abstract theme into an experience shared by author, subject, and reader would be to focus on what Johnson calls Savage's "first great Position, 'that Good is the Consequence of Evil,'" (*Savage*, p. 53). Before examining the complexity of this position within the *Life*, it might be well to consider some of Johnson's observations on this matter in his essays. In *Idler 89*, he remarks that "almost all the moral good which is left among us, is the apparent effect of physical evil," and he goes on to conclude his essay by noting, "That misery does not make all virtuous experience too certainly informs us; but it is no less certain that of what virtue there is, misery produces far the greater part." (2:276, 279). This statement, I believe, grows out of the general position that Johnson advances in *Rambler 70*, wherein he extends Hesiod's division of mankind into three orders of intellect to a division of mankind according to their morals. The first class of men includes those persons of such fixed principles that their life is steadfastly regulated by "the divine commands" and "the approbation of God." The third class includes those people whose life consists of immersion in pleasure and an abandonment "to passion without any desire of higher good." It is the second class, however, which Johnson asserts to be "so much the most numerous, that it may be considered as comprising the whole body of mankind." This class is described as follows: "There are others in a kind of equipoise between good and ill; who are moved on one part by riches or pleasure, by the gratifications of passion, and the delights of sense; and, on the other, by laws of which they own the obligation, and rewards of which they believe the reality, and whom a very small addition of weight turns either way" (*Rambler*, 4:3–4).

We should note, however, that even though Johnson does believe that good is often the consequence of evil, and that mankind on the whole lives in a state of "equipoise," straddling, as it were, good and evil, it is not enough for a writer simply to observe these facts and treat them as abstract themes. It is his responsibility to resist any deterministic interpretation, for such a deterministic view naturally leads to complacency and irresponsibility. Thus Johnson, even as he is agreeing with Savage's "first great Position," qualifies it and makes it more complicated, so that the reader will not succumb to the temptations that Johnson describes in *Rambler 4:* "For while men consider good and evil as springing from the same root, they will spare the one for the sake of the other, and in judging, if not of others at least of themselves, will be apt to estimate their virtues by their vices. To this fatal error all those will contribute, who confound the colours of right and wrong, and instead of helping to settle their boundaries, mix them with so much art, that no common mind is able to disunite them" (3:24).

Because Johnson is so preoccupied with what constitutes the "common mind"—both as pure cognition and as the exercise of moral choice—we should look for the following principles as they are embodied in the human experiences recorded in *The Life of Savage:* that good is often the consequence of evil because man exists in a state of equipoise between good and evil; that man is nevertheless a responsible moral agent; and that it is the writer's duty to "settle" the boundaries of good and evil in such a way that the reader's "common mind" is able to distinguish them. The key activities of mind which join the reader and Johnson are the processes of disuniting what is separable and adventitious and determining what is common to humankind. Together the reader and author sort out the reasons, causes, effects, virtues, and defects of Savage's life without, however, separating themselves from the essential, as opposed to adventitious, human bonds that the reader, author, and Savage share with one another as fellow human beings.

Indeed, the dominant mode both of style and structure in the *Life* is one of "equipoise," and it is because of this that the reader's simplistic expectations are so often anticipated and made complicated. For where we may be in the habit of seeing things as either/or—that is, reading the *Life* either skeptically or sentimentally—Johnson complicates our reading by continually calling attention to the complementary nature of apparent opposites. There is equipoise in a sentence such as this: "The two Powers which, in the Opinion of *Epictetus*, constituted a wise Man, are those of *bearing* and *forbearing*, which cannot indeed be affirmed to have been equally possessed by Savage; but it was too manifest that the Want of one obliged him very *frequently* to practise the other" (*Savage*, p. 126). Or Johnson writes that Savage "scarcely ever found a Stranger, whom he did not leave a friend, but it must likewise be added, that he had not a Friend long, without obliging him to become a Stranger" (*Savage*, p. 60). And this process of equipoise is often explicitly directed at the reader as a way of reminding us of how to read the *Life:* "Nor can his personal Example do any hurt, since whoever hears of his Faults, will hear of the Miseries which they brought upon him, and which would deserve less Pity, had not his Condition been such as made his Faults pardonable" (*Savage*, p. 75).

On a larger structural level, whenever one is tempted to think of Savage as purely a victim of circumstances, or as a man whom many people are "out to get," Johnson makes us aware of Savage's own deficiencies of character and reminds us that for every hostile person, such as Savage's purported mother or Judge Page, there is a Mr. Wilks or Mrs. Oldfield who respond to Savage with great compassion. Similarly, through the use of an apparently trivial detail Johnson makes the reader painfully aware of Savage's complicated state of mind, of his desire for resoluteness in the midst of irresolution. We are told, for example, that as a writer Savage "often altered, revised, recurred to his first Reading or Punctuation, and again adopted the Alteration; he was dubious and irresolute without End . . . the Intrusion or Omission of a Comma was sufficient to discompose him, and he would lament an Error of a single Letter as a heavy Calamity" (*Savage*, p. 58). Johnson is surely not just mocking Savage, nor making him an abstract type of indecision and ineffectuality. Rather, he has shown us how deeply Savage's irresolution runs, and yet how desperately (though unsuccessfully) Savage tries to exert some form of control, not just over his sentences, but over his life. But lest the reader too quickly extricate himself from Savage's circumstances, Johnson will extrapolate a general distinction from Savage's character so precisely and so forcefully that its equipoise stands as a danger signal provided for the reader's benefit—as, for example, in this sentence: "The reigning Error of his Life was, that he mistook the Love for the Practice of Virtue, and was indeed not so much a good Man, as the Friend of Goodness" (*Savage*, p. 74).

Moreover, if we do not acknowledge and exercise acts of "complicated Virtue," then Johnson at once dismisses our judgment and reproves our insensitivity: "Those are no proper Judges of his Conduct who have slumber'd away their Time on the Down of Plenty; nor will any wise Man easily presume to say, 'Had I been in *Savage's* Condition, I should have lived, or written, better than *Savage*'" (*Savage*, p. 140). The wisdom and judgment Johnson refers to emerge from his strenuous conviction that equipoise is the general state of mankind, and it is this conviction that entitles Johnson to expect and require the reader's ability to sort out the fundamentally human experience of Savage's life from the peculiarly individual events of his life. At one point in the *Life*, Johnson observes that "though there are few who will practise a laborious Virtue, there will never be wanting Multitudes that will indulge an easy Vice" (*Savage*, p. 68). The principal challenge of *The Life of Savage*—and it is characteristic of all of Johnson's writings —is that in order to understand and judge it we must practice "a laborious Virtue"—as readers, as critics, and as men.

Both in principle and in process, then, Johnson's use of biography is adjusted to the fallen state of man which he calls equipoise. But this principle and its corollary process of reader participation are far easier to enact in biography, which is a form of literature more closely aligned with the reader's sense of "reality," than in the apologue. Yet what Johnson says about the rise of the novel may, as well, be used to characterize biography: such a work exhibits "life in its true state, diversified only by accidents that daily happen in the world, and influenced by passions and qualities which are really to be found in conversing with mankind" (*Rambler*, 3:19). But what of a work like *Rasselas*, the apparent opposite in form of *The Life of Savage? Rasselas* does not attempt to take hold of the reader's imagination through what Johnson calls "historical veracity." Quite the contrary: its use of conspicuously fictional devices operates almost exclusively at a level of abstraction. *Rasselas* appears to conform readily to Sheldon Sacks's definition of an apologue: "a work organized as a fictional example of the truth of a formulable statement or a series of such statements." Thus Sacks argues, with the full endorsement of studies by Bertrand

Bronson and Gwin J. Kolb, that "stated in its most prosaic form, the concept obviously illustrated in *Rasselas* is that earthly happiness does not exist." [11]

Still, even on an abstract level there is some question as to whether *Rasselas* simply illustrates concepts or exercises activities and "motions" of mind. I do not mean to quibble, but there is tied to the notion of "illustration" an implied passivity, not to say futility, and yet the knowledge that earthly happiness does not exist, or more exactly does exist but is transient, seems to operate less as a theme than as the incontrovertible background against which Johnson's characters attempt to enact a variety of "choices of life." [12] We should recall, in this regard, that the original title of *Rasselas* was "The Choice of Life; or, The History of——Prince of Abissinia" (*Letters*, 1:117). Even if these enacted choices of life in *Rasselas* are not fully satisfactory, nor at times even partially satisfactory, they may nevertheless be acts of "complicated virtue," acts that generate correspondences in the reader's imagination, just as they evidently did in Johnson's mind. Boswell, after all, has reported Johnson to have remarked: "'Why sir,' said Johnson, 'the greatest concern we have in this world, the choice of our profession, must be determined without demonstrative reasoning. Human life is not yet so well known as that we can have it. And take the case of a man who is ill. I call two physicians: they differ in opinion. I am not to lie down, and die between them: I must do something'" (*Life*, 5:47). [13]

Just as Johnson *does* something, so do the characters in *Rasselas*, and so should the reader; and it is in the nature of these activities that they are done "without demonstrative reasoning." The trouble with reading *Rasselas* as if it were exclusively a fictional embodiment of an abstract principle is that it reduces the reader's experience, and the characters' experience as well, to a state bordering on paralysis. Moreover, such a concentration on abstract principle leaves the reader, and by implication Johnson, outside the work in a position of detached superiority with respect to the choices made by Johnson's characters. Such an attitude of cool observation, an attitude perhaps fed by some critics' confidence in the existence of "demonstrative reasoning," has led to such observations on *Rasselas* as that "the only rational 'choice of life' is the 'choice of eternity,' a 'mode of existence which shall furnish employment for the whole soul, and where pleasure shall be adequate to our powers of fruition'" [14] (which presumes that Nekayah is demonstrably right); another critic has asserted that "actually *Rasselas* is a vastly (if subtly) comic performance. . . . We can see that this tradition [the Oriental Tale] comes close to constituting an eighteenth-century version of Camp," and we are finally cautioned to observe, clearly from the vantage point of Manhood and Maturity, that "it has not always been noticed that the first sentence of *Rasselas* establishes it as virtually a boy's book."[15] These views reach their inevitable culmination in Arieh Sachs's statement that "this notion of a disengaged state of being, a notion directly derived from his personal need, guilt, and anguish, is the ideal Johnson sets up not only in his moral theories and as the goal of religious experience, but, in an important sense, as the point of departure for his literary criticism and aesthetic judgments as well."[16]

The notion of a "disengaged state of being" simply flies in the face of Johnson's description of his own understanding of humanity, as well as the narrative appeal of *Rasselas:* "In narratives, where historical veracity has no place, I cannot discover why there should not be exhibited the most perfect idea of virtue; of virtue not angelical, nor above probability, for what we cannot credit we shall never imitate, but the highest and purest that humanity can reach, which, exercised in such trials as the various revolutions of things shall bring upon it, may, by conquering some calamities, and enduring others, teach us what we may hope, and what we can perform" (*Rambler*, 3:24). It is not that I disagree, for example, with the observation that Johnson is frequently smiling in the background of *Rasselas*, but it is not the smile of comedy, mockery, or cynicism: it is a gesture of sympathetic understanding, a gesture that does not wholly detach Johnson either from his characters or from his readers, but attaches all of us in a series of common human predicaments.[17] W. K. Wimsatt has shrewdly noted the uniformity of the style of *Rasselas*—"the aphoristic moralisms, the lugubrious orotundity"—and the way all the characters speak in essentially the same mode. But the real point is that this style joins all the characters, separating out the essential from the adventitious, just as the moral content within this style joins the author and reader in a common language of humanity. In fact, there is a certain sense in which Imlac and Dr. Johnson occupy parallel positions: we know that Imlac has already engaged in wide travels and is a man of limited expectations, just as Johnson at this point in his life was not a man easily deluded. So there may be a limited sense in which Imlac is to the characters in *Rasselas* what Johnson is to the readers of *Rasselas:* namely, a man whose virtue has been "exercised in such trials as the various revolutions of things shall bring upon it," and who, "by conquering some calamities, and enduring others, [will] teach us what we may hope, and what we can perform." But even though Imlac and Johnson enjoy a position of some superiority, they continually speak the language of "we" and "us," not the language of "they" and "them."

The "veracity" of *Rasselas* is thus not, as in the *Life of Savage*, initially "historical," where the audience can immediately identify with a person in a reasonably familiar setting; rather it is continually cognitive and moral. We have already seen how Johnson, in the *Life of Savage*, deals with the motives and the psychology of one individual. No reader can emerge from the *Life of Savage* without a strong sense of how Savage's mind works. Now in *Rasselas* Johnson seems to be preoccupied with mind generally and with its principal mode of operation—the act of choice—which is an appropriate paradigm of reason. What Johnson does in *Rasselas* is to offer us a range of choices representing both the variety and uniformity of humanity. The variety is represented by the diversity of choices and individuals; but beneath this variety there exists a uniformity of mind and experience, a common desire to act virtuously which presumably joins the author, his characters, and the reader. The equipoise of *Rasselas* arises from the fact that though all the characters are vulnerable, they are nevertheless virtuous; taken together these two characteristics express the moral dilemmas of *Rasselas*. It is this very complication that prevents *Rasselas* from being predominantly comic or satiric, as I think we can see by examining some representative passages which initially presume judgment on the characters but which insist, finally, on the reader's compassionate exercise of self-examination.

A good model of Johnson's procedures in *Rasselas* is the episode with the learned astronomer. Many of the conventions of satire exist, at least in potential, within this episode. Indeed, the astronomer might have fit quite nicely in the Academy of Lagado of *Gulliver's Travels* except for the fact that Johnson is not writing a satire. The astronomer is crazy: he believes that he has possessed for "five years the regulation of weather, and the distribution of the seasons: the sun has listened to my dictates, and passed from tropick to tropick by my direction; the clouds, at my call, have poured their waters, and the Nile has overflowed at my command; I have restrained the rage of the dog-star, and mitigated the fervours of the crab."[18] If Johnson had left the episode at this, it would be easy to write off the astronomer as a lunatic; but despite his deluded belief, we learn in the next chapter that he has attempted to act virtuously, unlike the projectors in the Academy of Lagado. The astronomer, in other words, is exceedingly vulnerable—a characteristic that satire would capitalize on—but he is also virtuous, for we are reminded that despite the astronomer's "possession" of this power, and despite his own unhappiness in the belief that he has such power, "nothing but the consciousness of good intention could have enabled [him] to support the weariness of unremitted vigilance" (*Rasselas*, p. 110). Already, then, Johnson has begun the process of short-circuiting opportunities for the reader to dismiss the astronomer as a mere lunatic. But Johnson goes still further and creates a situation where reader response is objectified so as to establish a context for subsequent self-examination. Imlac finishes his story about the astronomer without comment, thus allowing us, as well as the characters, to form our own responses; and the characters do express a diversity of responses: "The prince heard this narration with very serious regard, but the princess smiled, and Pekuah convulsed herself with laughter" (*Rasselas*, p. 113). The question at this point is how do we, as readers, fit into this miniature spectrum of responses? Do we regard the story seriously, or do we, like the princess and Pekuah, either smile or convulse ourselves with laughter? The latter responses would certainly be appropriate to a comic or satiric reading, and they might also be the expected responses. But Imlac will have nothing to do with comedy or satire and immediately addresses himself to the ladies' responses: "'Ladies,' said Imlac, 'to mock the heaviest of human afflictions is neither charitable nor wise. Few can attain this man's knowledge, and few practise his virtues; but all may suffer his calamity. Of the uncertainties of our present state, the most dreadful and alarming is the uncertain continuance of reason'" (*Rasselas*, p. 113).

The rhetoric of Imlac's rejoinder—a characteristic rhetoric of *Rasselas*, I might add—is revealing: the contrast of "few" and "all" reverses conventional expectations concerning madness. At the beginning of the narrative it would appear that the astronomer, by virtue of being mad, should be classified among the "few"—just as lunatics are put into institutions out of general or "normal" society. The "all," of course, would be reserved for us normal people who, on the basis of our superior understanding, reserve the right to judge and eventually dismiss lunatics to the category of the "few." In his response to the ladies, however, Imlac reverses and thus complicates conventional formulations: the mad astronomer is among the "few," not because of his madness but because of his knowledge and his practice of virtue. On the other hand, the true bond he shares with us—"all" of us— is his calamity, for as Imlac later remarks, "Disorders of intellect . . . happen much more often than superficial observers will easily believe. Perhaps, if we speak with rigorous exactness, no human mind is in its right state" (*Rasselas*, pp. 113–16).

This episode of the learned astronomer, stretching over six short chapters (40–45), is calculated to address itself not just to the characters' but to the readers' tendency to be "superficial observers." What we assume to be stable and permanent, Johnson demonstrates to be fluctuating and transient. Our most basic assumptions are rendered problematical, just as Pekuah's ostensibly rational fear of and flight from the unknown, in the hopes of remaining safe, ironically lead to her kidnapping. Clearly, it is by the use of reason that we, much like the astronomer, believe that we can control our lives, or, like Pekuah, that we can rationally anticipate consequences. No man has been more identified with the exercise of reason than Samuel Johnson, and yet it is he who, altogether appropriately, insists on our consciousness of the limitations of reason, not as a satirist would do to lead the reader into a temporary paralysis of will, but to urge the necessity to act even, and perhaps primarily, when we are uncertain. Robert Voitle has observed that "the moral life is a life of constant activity. It is this belief that most decisively sets Johnson apart from those moralists who emphasize character and virtue."[19] This position can be extended into a critical framework describing Johnson's attempts to transform our customary reading habits of passive acceptance and observation into vigorous activity and participation. Many passages within the text of *Rasselas* not only batter home the theme of action but seem designed to stimulate the reader into activity.

The following passages, which are spread over the length of *Rasselas*, are dominated by the contrast between static observation and active participation, between forms of rational self-imprisonment and the necessary enactment of desire, however vulnerable it may be. Even the apparently foolish mechanical artist who attempts to fly and crashes into the water voices the dominant note of *Rasselas* when he asserts, "'Nothing . . . will ever be attempted, if all possible objections must be first overcome'" (*Rasselas*, p. 17). Or Imlac, a man who has known the life of activity and who voluntarily tries the sensual stasis of the Happy Valley, prods the characters into activity by continually reminding them of the complicated and insoluble nature of human needs and motives:

"Inconsistencies," answered Imlac, "cannot both be right, but imputed to man, they may both be true. Yet diversity is not inconsistency. My father [a man of great wealth] might expect a time of greater security. However, some desire is necessary to keep life in motion, and he, whose real wants are supplied, must admit those of fancy." (*Rasselas*, p. 21)

"The causes of good and evil," answered Imlac, "are so various and uncertain, so often entangled with each other, so diversified by various relations, and so much subject to accidents which cannot be foreseen, that he who would fix his condition upon incontestable reasons of preference, must live and die inquiring and deliberating." (*Rasselas*, pp. 46–47)

Or Nekayah, speaking on the subject of marriage and choosing a marriage partner, cautions Rasselas: "There are a thousand familiar disputes which reason never can decide: questions that elude investigation, and make logic ridiculous; cases where something must be done, and where little can be said. . . . Wretched would be the pair above all names of wretchedness, who should be doomed to adjust by reason every morning all the minute detail of a domestic day" (*Rasselas*, p. 77).

   What this all leads to—perhaps surprisingly—is not an assertion of irrationality or despair, but an ethic of activity based on a moral and psychological tolerance for and compassionate understanding of ambiguity, inconsistency, and uncertainty. In this regard there is a sense in which *The Life of Savage* is the specific example of which *Rasselas* is the general embodiment: both works approach, from varying literary perspectives, the human desire to enact choices that eventually fade into irresolution. But Johnson reminds us that it is woven into the fabric of life that such choices, though they do not assure stability, represent genuinely virtuous attempts to sustain life and to avoid paralysis and stagnation. Because Johnson is so preoccupied in *Rasselas* with the workings and needs of the human mind, he emphasizes compassionate understanding—his own, his characters', and his readers'—over abstract judgment, and sympathetic involvement over detached observation. What Imlac has to say about "our"—not "their"—minds in chapter 35 will later be both structurally and thematically enacted in Johnson's strangely indeterminate "conclusion":

> Our minds, like our bodies, are in continual flux; something is hourly lost, and something acquired. To lose much at once is inconvenient to either, but while the vital powers remain uninjured, nature will find the means of reparation. Distance has the same effect on the mind as on the eye, and while we glide along the stream of time, whatever we leave behind us is always lessening, and that which we approach increasing in magnitude. Do not suffer life to stagnate; it will grow muddy for want of motion: commit yourself again to the current of the world (*Rasselas*, p. 93).[20]

This passage is a pure example of Johnson's equipoise: it both describes and elicits a view that life is a process of loss and acquisition, of recollection and anticipation, of stagnation and motion, all of which occur within the flux that is called the "stream of time" and "the current of the world."

This view may explain why Samuel Johnson, a man known for his vigorous opinions and for a willingness to utter many pronouncements decisively and authoritatively, has himself chosen to end *Rasselas* with an unorthodox conclusion. If, indeed, *Rasselas* were the comedy or even satire that some readers have claimed it to be, one would reasonably expect a conclusion of some decisiveness. Instead we are presented with a conclusion that has caused consternation among readers chiefly because it is decisively indecisive. What we have is five characters in search of a conclusion within the formal context of a nonconclusive conclusion to an oriental tale. I have already spoken of Johnson's equipoise in the *Life of Savage*—of the delicate balancing evident within the events and style of Johnson's biography. But the conclusion of *Rasselas* pushes the experience of equipoise almost to its breaking point, mainly because we are not asked, as we are in the *Life of Savage*, to balance good against evil, nor virtue against vice. Rather, we are required to appreciate distinctions between competing acts of virtue and decisions among multiple choices of good, none of which will yield themselves to a more than temporary stability. The formal conclusion fluctuates, even as some of the characters attempt to impose decisions to arrest fluctuation. Pekuah wants to choose piety in the form of the convent of Saint Anthony, for she "would gladly be fixed in some unvariable state." Nekayah wants to choose learning and later establish "a college of learned women." Rasselas wants to choose government, wishing to be a philosopher-king, but "he could never fix the limits of his dominion, and was always adding to the number of his subjects." Appropriately, the older men (Imlac and the astronomer) "were contented to be driven along the stream of life without directing their course to any particular port."

Johnson has accomplished just what he talked about in *Rambler 4*. In writing an oriental tale, a narrative where "historical veracity has no place," he has exhibited characters of the highest and purest virtue that humanity can reach, and their choices of life certainly are the occasion for teaching us "what we may hope, and what we can perform." Amid the diversity of choices all the characters are collected into a community of virtue, and they return to Abissinia because their journey through many places has, in fact, been a journey of mind where place and rational control lose their expected importance, but where our understanding and appreciation of human "equipoise" gain in significance.

7
Sterne's Sixth Sense

There seems in some passages to want a sixth sense to do it rightly.—What can he mean by the lambent pupilability of slow, low, dry chat, five notes below the natural tone,— which you know, madam, is little more than a whisper?
                                        Lawrence Sterne, *Tristram Shandy*

We have seen how Johnson, particularly in *Rasselas*, accommodates his sense of "equipoise" to the uncertainties of human life. Such phrases as the "stream of time" and the "current of the world" evoke a sense of indeterminacy, and the narrative process of *Rasselas*, most dramatically its inconclusive conclusion, is obviously adjusted to the prevailing idea of being "contented to be driven along the stream of life without directing [our] course to any particular port." On the face of it, it might appear that the conclusion of *Rasselas* anticipates the whole of *Tristram Shandy*, for neither work is in any great hurry to arrive at any particular destination, but we know as well that Johnson is reported to have dismissed *Tristram Shandy* simply by saying, "Nothing odd will do long."[1] Clearly the oddity of *Tristram Shandy* represents a radical departure from Johnson's empirical understanding of the human mind, for Sterne, unlike Johnson, appeals to the reader's curiosity by transforming rationality, and its dependence on the world of the five senses, into a celebration of the world of the "sixth sense" which obliterates the moral and cognitive distinctions so basic to Johnson's idea of "equipoise."

To put it another way, all the authors I have examined thus far challenge the reader's rational expectations, but no work goes to the extremes of Sterne's novel. As Sterne writes, "If I thought you was able to form the least judgment or probable conjecture to yourself, of what was to come in the next page,—I would tear it out of my book."[2] (*TS*, 1:80). What this quotation, as well as the whole of *Tristram Shandy*, suggests is that the novel is one elaborate reading paradigm, explicitly designed to subvert the idea of the reader as detached observer; the mode of the paradigm is unique.

Customarily, novels are written in such a way that the reader is able to "form the least judgment or probable conjecture," and the reader is able to do so because novels ordinarily represent human beings performing familiar actions within familiar contexts. That is, readers observe human actions that are dependent on the five senses and determined by the coordinates of space and time. All of these customary props, if they may be called such, are either removed or minimized in *Tristram Shandy*. In their place Sterne substitutes a principle of indeterminacy, which should not be construed as an absence of meaning but rather as the plurality of meaning.[3]

Sterne writes, for example, "Observe, I determine nothing upon this.—My way is ever to point out to the curious, different tracts of investigation, to come at the first springs of the events I tell" (*TS*, 1:66); and near the end of his life he writes to Dr. John Eustace: "Your walking stick is in no sense more *shandaic* than in that of its having *more handles than one*—The parallel breaks only in this, that in using the stick, every one will take the handle which suits his convenience."[4] Here Sterne demonstrates his awareness of how we ordinarily read and how his book calls upon, and reeducates the reader towards, different reading processes. Confronted with a variety of choices—a number of handles, so to say—readers usually opt for one, the one that suits their convenience. If reading and writing are structuring activities of mind, then those activities tend to reduce the flux of experience to an apparently more stable singularity. That singularity, because it can be formulated, contained, and rationally inspected, we call meaning; but it is precisely this habit of specifying and observing that Sterne's novel resists. The reader may be closed-minded, for perfectly understandable reasons, but the book is open-ended, and our life as conventional readers is thereby "put in jeopardy by words" (*TS*, 1:87).

What is the difference, for instance, between a whisper and "the lambent pupilability of slow, low, dry chat, five notes below the natural tone?" A whisper is a word we recognize: it refers to an action we have performed and observed. The word is singular, it is referential, and it draws on our five senses. We feel we know its meaning. But what of the "lambent pupilability of slow, low, dry chat"? Is this phrase a synonym for whisper? Hardly. Instead of drawing on our ordinary senses it requires the reader to participate in, rather than simply recognize from memory, the processes of its meaning. The phrase lacks reference, but it invites us to activate our "sixth sense"— our imagination, as distinguished from our rational understanding. The meaning of the phrase exists in our imaginative experience of reading it—possibly reading it out loud. Our ordinary habits of reading words have been "put in jeopardy," which is to say that our customary reliance on the referential meaning of words has been challenged. Though we may feel threatened—the phrase is certainly odd—we may also be pleased: pleased because our imagination has been set free to roam among any number of possibilities.[5] The phrase does not so much describe a whisper as perform it. It whispers to our imagination by bypassing our rational understanding, and we perform its meaning. Perhaps we conjure up a woman to whom we would like to speak, or have spoken, in this way. It is not difficult to make the phrase sensual, though we need not insist on it. One could say that the cues are there, but they are there in no specifiable way. Assuming we know—and it is a huge assumption—what a "natural tone" is, we will have to imagine what "five notes" below the tone is. There is no way we can determine or measure our way "five notes below," but this very indeterminacy, at the moment it removes referential meaning, simultaneously activates the reader's imaginative experience.

In the same letter to Dr. John Eustace, Sterne writes that "a true feeler always brings half the entertainment along with him. His own ideas are only call'd forth by what he reads, and the vibrations within, so entirely correspond with those excited, 'tis like reading *himself* and not the *book*" (*Letters*, p. 411). The vibrations emanating from the author's and reader's imagination are the sixth sense to which Sterne continually appeals. The imagination feeds on the five senses, but it is not bound by them. To experience vibrations the reader must let go— must release himself from the dominance of the five senses and the coordinates of space and time. The imagination is without place, without time, unrestricted by the five senses, and hence indeterminate. It is its own world, a world of vibrations, but these vibrations may only be experienced to the extent that reader and author abandon the props of their ordinary habits and expectations. In this regard, the oddity of *Tristram Shandy* is that it is not simply a conventional story "about" Tristram, Uncle Toby, Walter, Yorick, Trim, Widow Wadman, and the rest. Rather, it is the imaginative experience of writing and reading the experiences that are the indeterminate processes of their imaginations. *Tristram Shandy* is thus not so much *about* the life and opinions of Tristram Shandy as it *is* the life and opinions. The book is so calculated to defy our ordinary reading habits that it dissolves the most basic of literary distinctions—that between the reader and the book. As James Swearingen has persuasively argued, Tristram's "ideal requires that both he and his reader abandon themselves and their methods of procedure to the free play of the event in which new meanings unpredictably occur."[6] If it is true, as Sterne suggests, that for the reader who is a "true feeler" the act of reading *Tristram Shandy* is "like reading *himself* and not the *book*," then this very dissolution also opens up the vibratory experience of the reader's sixth sense which Sterne continually appeals to.

Speaking of the problem of reality in Sterne, John Traugott has noted that "there is a very great consciousness in the reader, and in the writer as well, of this problem of reality—what it is. And this is something that does not appear, it seems to me, in other eighteenth-century writers."[7] I agree completely with this statement. The reader's ordinary sense of reality is made problematical in large measure because Sterne, as I have suggested, removes the conventional props of the five senses and the coordinates of space and time; hence the seeming oddity that Johnson notes in Sterne's fiction. Because Sterne activates the reader's consciousness of the problematical nature of reality—to the point, perhaps, that "Tristram's whole enterprise is a hermeneutics, a process of self-interpretation"[8]—he is frequently thought of as a "modern" writer; for Sterne's sense of reality is strangely akin to the more recent fiction of Joyce, Beckett, Pynchon, Vonnegut, Borges, and Barth. The term "modern," however, unless in some way specified, can become simply an honorific term, a way of appropriating and congratulating alleged precursors. By "modern" I mean to designate no single historical period, but rather a characteristic method of a certain kind of writing which Gabriel Josipovici describes as "an insistence on the fact that what previous generations had taken for *the world* was only *the world seen through the spectacles of habit.*"[9]

If we examine Josipovici's formulation, it has a striking resemblance to Sterne's authorial procedures. What Josipovici describes as "the world" is the conventional view of reality, or what philosophers call "naïve realism." This is a view which since the late seventeenth century, at least, has passed for the world of reason and common sense.

Novels written in accordance with this view tend either to assume the existence of, or represent, an external world that is stable, verifiable, and familiar. These "spectacles of habit," or what Howard Anderson examines through Sterne's "parables of preconception," function analogously to Sterne's hobbyhorses.[10] The "modern" view, however, is less preoccupied with the world so-called than with the constitutive power of individual perception.

Indeed, the characters in *Tristram Shandy* represent a spectrum of perceptual models.[11] Instead of a world, Sterne presents the reader with a series of worlds, governed by the characters' particular hobbyhorses. To these worlds, the reader, if he is a true feeler, contributes his own spectacles of habit. Only insofar as the reader's experience of *Tristram Shandy* is measured against the norms of ordinary reality, or conventional story-telling, is it chaotic. If, on the other hand, the novel is read in light of Sterne's principle of letting *"people tell their stories their own way"* (*TS*, 9:633), then the overall effect is to break down the familiar world of rational distinctions in order to activate the sixth sense of the reader's and writer's imagination. What from a conventional point of view indisputably appears to be an odd book with characters seemingly isolated from "reality" becomes, in the context of Sterne's appeal to the reader's sixth sense, "a strangely effective [symbol] of liberty operating in the world of necessity," to quote Lionel Trilling.[12]

Thus it is that Sterne chooses to write not only the life but the opinions of Tristram Shandy. The life alone, as fictional biography or autobiography, would usually proceed in a linear movement from birth to death or the approach of death. This linear movement would conform to the conventions of ordinary reality. That is, the emphasis would be primarily on actions performed, on the events of life seen in retrospect and, for all intents and purposes, completed. These actions, moreover, would be observed in familiar social contexts bound by the coordinates of space and time. On the other hand, opinions do not necessarily conform to a linear time scheme, for they are as much, if not more, a part of interior time—the time of the mind rather than the time of public life. Opinions make up their own interior history, a history heedless of cause and effect, space and time, and the boundaries of the five senses. The paradox is that life and opinions go on simultaneously, but they are not necessarily interconnected. In a sense, the life is a history of the body, while the opinions are the history of the mind; and though they may influence one another, they may also carry on separate existences. It is precisely this doubleness that Sterne juggles throughout *Tristram Shandy*, and which the reader must abandon himself to if he is to experience the liberating effects of Sterne's appeal to our imagination. Like Sterne, the reader must read the book not just from the point of view of his own public life, but in light of his own opinions as well. Sterne not only "whispers" to us; he speaks to our imagination in a "slow, low, dry chat, five notes below the natural tone." Thus the book becomes less an object that we observe than a process that we participate in. The book, as Sterne suggested to Dr. John Eustace, becomes the reader, and the reader, on exercising the sixth sense of his own imagination, ends up reading himself just as the book reads the reader.

If it is evidence that a skeptical reader requires, Sterne provides numerous passages in *Tristram Shandy* in which he attempts to educate the reader into a wholly new process of reading. The novel is laced with what I call reading paradigms. These paradigms at once encourage, if they do not require, the reader to abandon his ordinary reading habits, at the same time that Sterne appeals to the vibratory experiences of imagination which will be the bridge joining the reader and the author. In this regard, Sigurd Burckhardt has suggested that the element "common to bridges, ballistics, story lines and writing. . . . is that of 'getting something across,' whether it is missiles or people or meanings. . . . nothing seems so obvious to [Sterne]—and nothing should *be* so obvious—as that, if you want to project something over a gap, your line can never be straight, but must be inclined, parabolic, hyperbolic, cycloid."[13]

This is how Sterne appeals to the true feeler's sixth sense, but the reader and author, who initially approach one another as strangers, must first become friends:

In the beginning of the last chapter, I inform'd you exactly *when* I was born; but I did not inform you, *how*. No; that particular was reserved entirely for a chapter by itself;—besides, Sir, as you and I are in a manner perfect strangers to each other, it would not have been proper to have let you into too many circumstances relating to myself all at once.—You must have a little patience. I have undertaken, you see, to write not only my life, but my opinions also; hoping and expecting that your knowledge of my character, and of what kind of a mortal I am, by the one, would give you a better relish for the other: As you proceed further with me, the slight acquaintance which is now beginning betwixt us, will grow into familiarity; and that, unless one of us is in fault, will

terminate in friendship. . . . Therefore, my dear friend and companion, if you
should think me somewhat sparing of my narrative on the first setting out,—
bear with me,—and let me go on, and tell my story my own way. (*TS*,
1:10–11)

What does it mean, and imply, when Sterne says, "and let me go
on, and tell my story my own way"? For one thing, it means that
Sterne is completely aware of the reader's initial sense of disorientation.
It means that he knows, and wants us to know, that to perform a reading of the novel we must first abandon our established reading habits
and expectations, and that we must trust the author, as well as our own
imaginations. We may know more than we are conscious of. Sterne
knows that we feel like strangers because the props of friendship normally established by authors—those props being the five senses and the
coordinates of space and time—are in the process of being removed.
We have been told when Tristram was born, which conforms with our
conventional need to know, but we have not been told how, though
eventually this will occur. How and when are ordinarily interrelated,
but Sterne is already beginning to split them up. A novel about "when"
would have much to say about public life, about cause and effect, but
Sterne is more interested in "how," particularly as it relates to opinion,
or the interior life of the mind. The journey metaphor that is evident
throughout *Tristram Shandy* serves to show that the "whens" of conventional fiction—also the "wheres"—necessarily recede into the
"hows" of Sterne's imagination.

The conventional use of the journey appears repeatedly as an organizing principle in eighteenth-century fiction. Fielding, Defoe, Smollett, Johnson, and Godwin all use it, though they use it in a variety
of ways, ranging from the purely social to the psychological and
spiritual. Sterne, however, uses it in at least two uniquely different
ways. First, Sterne thinks of the journey in an almost exclusively interior manner. In volume 7, for example, Tristram travels to flee death,
but the external travel is important only as it occasions the interior pur-
suits of Tristram's mind. Tristram's concern for his own physical life,
in other words, excites the interior life of his opinions. He is less preoccupied with external observations of the wheres and whens of his
travel than with the reflections of his own mind as he travels; and these
reflections, because they are not governed by external time or place, are
therefore timeless and become their own place. How radically Sterne

conceives of the imagination's absorption of external time and place may be seen in the following passage:

I have been getting forwards in two different journies together, and with the same dash of the pen—for I have got entirely out of *Auxerre* in this journey which I am writing now, and I am got half way out of *Auxerre* in that which I shall write hereafter. . . . I have brought myself into such a situation, as no traveller ever stood before me; for I am this moment walking across the market-place of *Auxerre* with my father and my uncle *Toby,* in our way back to dinner—and I am this moment also entering *Lyons* with my post-chaise broke into a thousand pieces—and I am moreover this moment in a handsome pavillion built by *Pringello,* upon the banks of the *Garonne.* (*TS,* 7:515–16)

In this passage the "when" of Tristram's travels is played against the "how." The passage tantalizes the reader with seemingly external references to place—Auxerre, Lyons, Garonne—and yet the how of Sterne's imagination enables him to be in three places at once. The co-ordinates of space and time have been blithely annulled in a way that no other fictional journey in eighteenth-century fiction either attempts or dreams about. Moreover, Sterne has so scrambled tenses that the purported events of past and future, on which the reader customarily determines "the least judgment or probable conjecture," have been anticipated and undercut by the dominance of Sterne's irregular but imaginative use of the present tense. Just as Sterne defies the reader's reliance on the five senses, so he scuttles the conventional uses of tense. Tristram is entirely out of Auxerre in the journey about which he is presently writing, he is half way out of Auxerre in a future journey, and at the same time that he is in Auxerre he is also entering Lyons, as well as being in a pavilion on the banks of the Garonne. This is a clear defiance of time, of what the reader ordinarily thinks of as reality. It is certainly odd, but it is not crazy.

What such a passage both requires and encourages in the reader is an abandonment of ordinary reading habits and expectations, along with the reader's activation of his own sixth sense. The reader's imagination is liberated, as Trilling puts it, "in the world of necessity." Sterne's imagination simply will not be bound, for it exists in its own interior place, just as it absorbs all exterior places. His continual insistence on "I am" is an exact linguistic analogue to the reader's experience of time in *Tristram Shandy.* As Jean-Jacques Mayoux has shrewdly observed about Sterne: "It has been the characteristic effort of his admirable willfulness to blend and confuse the time-structure of the story with the time infrastructure of the writing. . . . His writing . . . is a sort of conversation, not so much between the characters as between the author and the reader in yet another present, the time of their imaginary meeting." [14] This "yet another present," the time of our imaginary meeting, is the world of what I have called the sixth sense, where the singular life of rational observation recedes into the plural effects of the reader's imagination. The question is, How can Sterne's "I am" overcome the apparent barriers of the reader's expectations in such a way as to mesh with and activate the reader's sense of "I am"? Here we return to the problem that Sterne earlier poses: namely, how will we readers, as strangers, become Sterne's friend?

The key word is "become," and this leads to Sterne's second highly original use of the journey metaphor. *Tristram Shandy* is not so much a description of a journey, nor is it so much organized by a journey, as it *is* a journey that the reader participates in. The journey is completely identified with the process of writing and reading *Tristram Shandy*, and in this sense the journey is no longer a metaphor. It is a process of identity. In Sterne's terms, as strangers we read the book as if it were an external journey—the history of Tristram's life and the life of the Shandy household. But as friends or companions, we are, by virtue of the sixth sense of our imagination, active participants in the journey, and thus no longer separable from the interior journey of Tristram's life and opinions. This is how the reader, to use Sterne's terms, is invited to read not only the book but himself. We read ourselves when the journey is no longer seen as a metaphor organizing the book, but as the experience joining the reader, author, and book in a process of mutual identification, or what Burckhardt calls the "cycloid curve." The net effect of this process of experience is to dissolve past and future and to lead the reader into an experience of a continuous present, the experience of "I am," set in the unique time of the imaginary meeting of the reader, author, and book.

A wonderful example of how deliberately Sterne creates a unique sense of time occurs when he discusses the several ways of writing a travel narrative. He distinguishes between those "*who have wrote and gallop'd* or who have *gallop'd and wrote*, which is a different way still; or who for more expedition than the rest, have *wrote-galloping*, which is the way I do at present" (*TS*, 7:482). Here Sterne is playing with the conventional distinction between the act of writing and the experi-

ence that writing ostensibly represents. This distinction grows out of the
familiar formulation of fiction as imitation—novels, for example, as a
realistic imitation of individual actions in social reality. There is the act
of imitation (what authors have "wrote") and the action represented (the
experiences drawn from having "gallop'd"). Such a distinction, seen as
a formula for writing, presumes any number of further distinctions, not
the least of which is the separation between the perceiver and the
perceived, and between observation and participation. That is, we are
not to identify the author with the book, nor are we to regard the book
as anything other than a representation. Moreover, such a distinction
presumes sequence; there is first one thing, then another. Writing and
galloping thus cannot occur simultaneously because such a distinction
presumes a unilinear sense of time, something akin to cause and effect,
or what Aristotle calls the beginning, middle, and end.

   But as soon as Sterne declares that his way is to "write-galloping"
all these conventional distinctions instantly dissolve. They dissolve
because they are irrelevant. The book is a journey that identifies the
reader and the act of reading with the author and the act of writing.
We are all in it together by virtue of the time of our imaginary meeting.
The book is the occasion for the conjunction of the reader's time and the
author's time, and that time is one of a continuous present and continuous possibility. There is no before or after, no beginning or end: it
is all now and in the middle. The hyphen in the term "wrote-galloping"
is an enactment of the process joining the reader, author, and book.
The acts of writing and reading *are* the book, for the book is, rather
than represents, experience. This sense of an unfolding present, as expressed by the hyphen, is no less evident in Sterne's use of the dash,
about which Ian Watt has remarked: "Sterne's affront to conventional
syntax is essential to establishing the qualities he required for Tristram's
voice: Sterne didn't want unity or coherence or defined direction,
at least in any conventional sense; he wanted multiplicity, not unity;
he wanted free association of ideas, not subordination of them; he
wanted to go backwards or forwards or sideways, not in straight linear
patterns." [15]

   If Sterne "wrote-galloping," then the reader, if he is a true feeler,
"reads-galloping." There is, in other words, no essential separation
between the activities of writing and reading and the experience of what
is written and read. Sterne overcomes conventional distinctions, just as
he defies conventional syntax, by continually halving matters, which is

how the reader and author, as apparent strangers, grow to become companions and friends. As Sterne writes:

Writing, when properly managed, (as you may be sure I think mine is) is but a different name for conversation. As no one, who knows what he is about in good company, would venture to talk all;—so no author, who understands the just boundaries of decorum and good breeding, would presume to think all: The truest respect which you can pay to the reader's understanding, is to halve this matter amicably, and leave him something to imagine, in his turn, as well as yourself.

For my own part, I am eternally paying him compliments of this kind, and do all that lies in my power to keep his imagination as busy as my own. (*TS*, 2:108–9)

The reader's imagination is kept busy because Sterne, in halving matters, strictly speaking never finishes anything. He doesn't finish anything because the world of imagination and opinion, as distinguished from the life of ordinary reality, is ongoing and unrestricted by the five senses and the coordinates of space and time. The "place" where Sterne and the reader meet is in the imagination, which makes it no less real, but which does make matters a good deal less determinate. There is, however, a peculiar sense of completion which occurs when the reader and author halve matters. This completion, or act of friendship, happens when the reader and author participate within one another's imagination. The process of halving matters, which looks like an act of separation, is accomplished, paradoxically, so that the author and reader can put it together.

For example, the typographical and organizational conventions of a book's physical appearance, which conventions are designed to promote the illusion of a book as a representation of a sequential action, are continually violated in *Tristram Shandy*.[16] The book, we are frequently reminded, is not a representation of an action so much as it is the pure activity of imagination, freed from the bounds of convention. The reader is presented with a blank page that we are invited to fill in, with chapters deliberately out of numerical sequence, with a preface that appears in the third volume, with a marbled page that serves as a "motly emblem" of the novel (*TS*, 3:226), with a black page following Yorick's death, with the formal beginning of Tristram's "Life and Opinions" occurring in volume 4, chapter 32, and with the whole novel concluding five years before Tristram's birth. In addition, Sterne frequently uses series of asterisks and lines of dashes, as well as a variety of plot diagrams (i.e., *TS*, 6:473–74), all of which defy straight lines and the conventions they symbolize. The effect of all this scrambling of the physical appearance of the book is to turn it into a precursor of a Rorschach test, where the reader ends up reading himself.

Moreover, even a cursory look at the book's interpolated stories demonstrates another version of how Sterne "halves" conventional matters. These interpolated tales—Trim's sermon in volume 2, the announcement of Bobby's death in volume 4, the story of Le Fever in volume 6, the story of the King of Bohemia and his seven castles in volume 8—are all at least repeatedly interrupted, and either are left unfinished, or are so interrupted that their conclusions are anticlimactic. The interruptions are the necessary intrusions of the imagination, or the interior life of opinions, into the ostensibly hard data of life. Every one of these interruptions is an exercise and declaration of the life and freedom of the imagination. Even the story of the amours of Uncle Toby and Widow Wadman does not so much finish as fizzle. Widow Wadman's preoccupation with Toby's body disables her sixth sense. She wants to enact completion; she wants to possess Toby's body if it is in good repair; but her impulses are precisely those of a conventional reader (as opposed to a true feeler) who both assumes and wishes to impose the laws of the physical world onto the life of Toby's imagination.

But to finish a story, evidently, is to "kill" an experience, for the act of completion is the cessation of imagination. This idea leads to another conventional distinction—that between art and life—which Sterne repeatedly defies and dissolves. Critics have debated for years, with no promise, significantly, of resolution, the questions of whether Tristram is a persona or Sterne himself, and whether the novel is in any formal sense complete or unfinished. These questions are irrelevant, for they presume the existence of definite, verifiable answers in the face of the novel's overwhelming indeterminacy. Such questions also assume a reading of the book as an object for observation, rather than an experience of the conjunction of the reader's and writer's imaginations. But Sterne, both in the novel and in his correspondence, demolishes the distinction between art and life, and instead identifies art and life as a symbiotic process. This identity of art and life is necessary to preserve an "openness toward the future,"[17] and one way to see this is to consider Sterne's many declarations of art as life. First from *Tristram Shandy:*

In short, there is no end of it. . . . [I shall] go on leisurely, writing and publishing two volumes of my life every year;—which, if I am suffered to go on quietly, and can make a tolerable bargain with my bookseller, I shall continue to do as long as I live. (*TS*, 1:37)

I have constructed the main work and the adventitious parts of it with such intersections . . . that the whole machine, in general, has been kept a-going;—and, what's more, it shall be kept a-going these forty years, if it pleases the fountain of health to bless me so long with life and good spirits. (*TS*, 1:73–74)

Don't be exasperated, if I pass it by again with good temper,—being determined as long as I live or write (which in my case means the same thing) never to give the honest gentleman a worse word or a worse wish. (*TS*, 3:162)

The more I write, the more I shall have to write—and consequently, the more your worships read, the more your worships will have to read. . . . was it not that my OPINIONS will be the death of me, I perceive I shall lead a fine life of it out of this self-same life of mine. . . . I shall never overtake myself. (*TS*, 4:286)

But this is neither here nor there—why do I mention it?—Ask my pen,—it governs me,—I govern not it. (*TS*, 6:416)

For my own part, I am resolved never to read any book but my own, as long as I live. (*TS*, 8:544)

Although the context of the above passages changes, the content—namely, that art and life are inseparable—does not. And in his correspondence Sterne continues in a similar vein. He writes that *Tristram Shandy* is "a picture of myself, and so far may bid the fairer for being an Original" (*Letters*, p. 87); that "I shall write as long as I live, 'tis, in fact, my hobby-horse" (*Letters*, p. 143); that "I must take up again the pen.—In faith I think I shall die with it in my hand" (*Letters*, p. 277); and, echoing *Tristram Shandy*, 6:416, that "the truth is this—that my pen governs me—not me my pen" (*Letters*, p. 394). All of these assertions express Sterne's firm conviction that "an author must feel himself, or his reader will not" (*Letters*, p. 402).

Moreover what follows from Sterne's assertions is simply this: that life is opinion is imagination is the book is the author is the reader is life, ad infinitum. This is not the absence of meaning; it is the enclosure of meaning in a space—the sixth sense of imagination—that embraces and absorbs everything. The book is perpetual motion—what Coleridge calls the "infinite I am";[18] for motion is life, and, like Sterne's digressions, motion is the "sunshine . . . the life, the soul of reading" (*TS*, 1:73). Toby Olshin has summed up the process very nicely: "It is this self-justifying surge of life, independent of all need for external meaning, that Sterne celebrates."[19] But to be separated from our customary reliance on the props of external meaning is surely to be disoriented—to be made to feel odd. Does not Sterne run the risk of making us strangers at the same time that he tells his readers, "I beg only you will make no strangers of yourselves, but sit down without any ceremony, and fall on heartily" (*TS*, 2:84)? Yes, he runs the risk, but he has repeatedly shown the reader ways to overcome it. We can overcome the apparent isolation and chaos of *Tristram Shandy* if we abandon the props of ceremony—our strict reliance on reason—and "fall on heartily" with our imagination.

Still, if at every step in *Tristram Shandy* "the judgment is surprised by the imagination" (*TS*, 8:539), some strange consequences follow. For one thing, the world of contradiction—which is determined by the physical laws of the five senses, the coordinates of space and time, and the logical law of the excluded middle—gives way to the indeterminate world of the sixth sense, the conjunction of the writer's and reader's imaginations. The result, to borrow a title from one of John Barth's books, is that the reader is lost in the funhouse; or to invoke a title from Borges, we enter the world of labyrinths. Sterne is acutely aware of this when he observes, "What nonsense it is, either in fighting, or writing, or any thing else (whether in rhyme to it, or not) which a man has occasion to do—to act by plan" (*TS*, 8:575). Sterne provides an even better paradigm and analogue to the appeal of his book when he talks about knots: "In the case of these *knots* then, and of the several obstructions, which, may it please your reverences, such knots cast in our way in getting through life—every hasty man can whip out a penknife and cut through them.—'Tis wrong. Believe me, Sirs, the most virtuous way, and which both reason and conscience dictate—is to take our teeth or our fingers to them. . . . I shall never get the knots untied as long as I live" (*TS*, 3:168).

We, too, will never get the knots untied—so long, that is, as we acknowledge that the world of imagination is not the world of hasty men whipping out their penknives. To cut into a knot, or a book, is to cut through it. To take our teeth or fingers to a knot, or a book, is to become a part of it, as Sterne wishes us to do. Sterne, like another modern author, Thomas Pynchon, writes for "true feelers" (Pynchon calls them "sensitives"). And what Pynchon says about *Gravity's Rainbow* applies with equal force to the reader's participation in *Tristram Shandy:* "No, this is not a disentanglement from, but a progressive *knotting into*." [20]

8
Moral and Tendency
in 'Caleb Williams'

*I will write a tale, that shall constitute an epoch in the mind
of the reader, that no one, after he has read it, shall ever
be exactly the same man that he was before.*
                    William Godwin, *Caleb Williams*

It is true, as some critics have shown, that *Caleb Williams* may
be read to some extent as an analysis of the corrupting influences
of social and political institutions, but such a reading is unable
to account for the compelling psychological reverberations of the
novel.[1] Because Godwin uses a reading model by which the internal workings of the imagination, activated by Caleb's curiosity,
elicit a fascinating sense of psychological complicity, I believe
that *Caleb Williams* is the most insistently psychological novel
to be considered in this study.

Godwin, as the original preface (which was withdrawn) of the
novel indicates, initially intended his work to be a fictional embodiment of his own political interests—a kind of follow-up to
his earlier *Enquiry;* but Godwin also knew that social and political
institutions are themselves expressions of the latent fears and desires of the human mind. *Caleb Williams* simply does not deal
exclusively with social injustice, a topic that would result in a
political melodrama where the reader oscillates between praise
and accusation.[2] Rather it deals with human culpability and vulnerability, and the psychological experiences enacted by the characters lure the reader into turning inward to the complexities of
his own and the characters' mental processes.

In his essay "Of Choice in Reading," Godwin distinguishes
between the moral of a literary work and its tendency, using the
Iliad, Gulliver's Travels, Paradise Lost, The Fair Penitent, and
Richardson's characterization of Lovelace and Grandison (i.e.,

"It would not perhaps be adventurous to affirm that more readers have
wished to resemble Lovelace, than have wished to resemble Grandison") as examples of how the moral and the tendency of a work may be
antithetical to one another. From these examples Godwin offers the
following observations:

The moral of any work may be defined to be that ethical sentence to the illustration of which the work may most aptly be applied. The tendency is the actual
effect it is calculated to produce upon the reader, and cannot be completely
ascertained but by the experiment. . . . From the distinctions here laid down it
seems to follow, that the moral of a work is a point of very subordinate con-
sideration, and that the only thing worthy of much attention is the tendency.
It appears not unlikely that, in some cases, a work may be fairly susceptible
of no moral influence, or none but a bad one, and yet may have a tendency in
a high degree salutary and advantageous. . . . The principal praise is certainly
due to those authors, who have a talent to "create a soul under the ribs of
death," whose composition is fraught with irresistible enchantment; who pour
their whole souls into mine, and raise me as it were to the seventh heaven; who
furnish me with "food for contemplation even to madness"; who raise my
ambition, expand my faculties, invigorate my resolutions and seem to double
my existence.[3]

Tendency, in other words, translates as the psychological appeal by
which the reader participates in the fullness of a work's meaning; and
there is no question that Richardson would be appalled, but perhaps not
surprised, by Godwin's observations on Lovelace and Grandison. Tendency is that sort of imaginative transaction which supersedes the
claims of purely rational observation, and which deals exclusively with
psychological effect. The supreme embodiment of tendency in *Caleb
Williams* is Caleb himself, who initially wishes to function as a moral
observer, but who rapidly becomes the surrogate reader—the basic
principle of curiosity—who enacts experiences which the reader reenacts. In the same essay, Godwin writes: "Curiosity [Caleb's singular
mental characteristic] is one of the strongest impulses of the human
heart. To curiosity it is peculiarly incident to grow and expand itself
under difficulties and opposition. The greater are the obstacles to its
being gratified, the more it seems to swell, and labour to burst the
mounds that confine it" (*ENQ*, p. 131).

What I am suggesting, therefore, is that *Caleb Williams* is singularly preoccupied with the "epoch of mind"—the psychological encoun-

ter with fears and desires—of which social and political institutions are the most visible manifestation. Caleb is both the vehicle of and a participant in Godwin's essentially psychological exploration. He is a principle of curiosity: "The spring of action which, perhaps more than any other, characterized the whole train of my life, was curiosity. . . . I was desirous of tracing the variety of effects which might be produced from given causes. . . . I could not rest until I had acquainted myself with solutions that had been invented for the phenomena of the universe." [4] Caleb also excites the reader's curiosity, and as a participant in the novel's actions he expresses the desires of the reader's curiosity which, in the face of numerous obstacles, necessarily grow and expand "under difficulties and opposition."

If there is a metaphor that operates as the reading paradigm of the novel's psychological tendency, it is Falkland's trunk, whose contents are never explicitly revealed, whose contents Falkland and Caleb are obsessed with, and whose implicit meaning is the subject and stimulus of Caleb's and the reader's curiosity. The trunk appears at three significant moments—once in each volume—and at each appearance it accrues increased psychological meaning. Like the reader, Caleb becomes preoccupied with the contents of the trunk. The trunk stimulates Caleb's curiosity: that is, it stirs not only his desire to discover its meaning, but, failing that, his need to attach meaning to it. At the beginning of the novel Caleb, who is Falkland's secretary, goes to Falkland's room and as he opens the door

I heard at the same instant a deep groan expressive of intolerable anguish. The sound of the door in opening seemed to alarm the person within; I heard the lid of a trunk hastily shut, and the noise as of fastening a lock. I conceived that Mr. Falkland was there, and was going instantly to retire; but at that moment a voice that seemed supernaturally tremendous, exclaimed, "Who is there?" The voice was Mr. Falkland's. The sound of it thrilled my very vitals. I endeavoured to answer, but my speech failed, and being incapable of any other reply I instinctively advanced within the door into the room. . . . "Villain!" cried he, "what has brought you here?" I hesitated a confused and irresolute answer. "Wretch!" interrupted Mr. Falkland, with uncontrollable impatience, "you want to ruin me. You set yourself as a spy upon my actions; but bitterly shall you repent your insolence. Do you think you shall watch my privacies with impunity?" I attempted to defend myself. "Begone, devil!" rejoined he. "Quit the room, or I will trample you into atoms." (*CW*, p. 8)

Caleb and Falkland are each stunned by the other's presence, and the passage suggests that each is interpreting the other in light of some compulsive desire either to project onto, or defend himself from, the other's presence. Caleb is continually, and I would say compulsively, attaching meaning to Falkland's appearance, gesture, and sound, as if he were shaping Falkland to satisfy some inner psychological necessity. Falkland's groan, he believes, is "expressive of intolerable anguish," his voice seems "supernaturally tremendous," the lid of the trunk is "hastily shut," and Caleb's vitals are "thrilled." Caleb is as much projecting meaning onto Falkland as he is describing what occurs. Falkland does the same thing: Caleb is a "villain," a "Wretch," a "devil," and Falkland threatens to "trample" him, all this without Caleb having uttered a word. It seems fair to ask why such a seemingly mundane event produces such intense emotion; the event is calculated to elicit this question not only from Caleb and Falkland, but from the reader as well. The trunk is the focus of the encounter, and the reactions of the characters begin to arouse the reader's interest in its contents. No specific meaning is attached to the trunk, and yet its affective appeal is striking. Indeed, immediately after his encounter with Falkland, Caleb relates this event to Mr. Collins, who in turn tells Caleb the history of Falkland's past, which narration occupies the whole of volume 1. It is as if Collins's narration is to serve as a provisional, but finally unsatisfactory, answer to the question, "What is in the trunk?"

One sentence in this passage is peculiarly apposite to Caleb's subsequent behavior and to the development of the novel's psychological tendency: "I endeavoured to answer, but my speech failed, and being incapable of any other reply, I instinctively advanced within the door into the room." Although Caleb at this point is speechless, all of his activities in the remainder of the novel are governed by his compulsive desire to raise the contents of the trunk from obscurity to the level of meaningful speech. Caleb cannot psychologically tolerate the absence of meaning: his curiosity, like the reader's, requires—indeed, feeds on —meaning. In Caleb's world secrets must become public, not merely to satisfy his curiosity, but to defend his obsessive attachment to the idea that all human activity is rationally accessible and that all human problems are soluble. The other important point of this sentence is the phrase: "I instinctively advanced within the door into the room." Caleb's curiosity is not entirely governed by conscious control: his instincts exceed his control and always drive him forward. This attribute is not only necessary as a narrative device for providing interest and momentum; it is a psychological attribute by which the reader is lured into reenacting Caleb's mental processes. The meaning of the novel is in the experience of Caleb's pursuit of meaning, rather than at the end of his rational inquiry. Successive appearances of the trunk neither progressively refine on nor cancel the prior meanings attached to the trunk. It is all part of a dynamic process of flight and pursuit, an interior journey of mind precipitated by exterior events but governed by inner psychological necessity.

In volume 2 a fire breaks out on Falkland's estate, and in Falkland's absence Caleb rightly takes the responsibility of looking after the emergency. Once again, however, Caleb's actions are governed less by the immediate fact of the fire than by his preoccupation with the contents of the trunk. By this time Caleb strongly suspects that Falkland is the murderer of Squire Tyrrel; his curiosity, in other words, appears to be motivated by a specific intent, and he is convinced that the contents of the trunk will prove his case. Nevertheless, his interest in the trunk, as the passage suggests, is governed by more than a simple desire for justice:

My steps, by some mysterious fatality, were directed to the private apartment at the end of the library. Here, as I looked round, my eye was suddenly caught by the trunk mentioned in the first pages of my narrative. My mind was already raised to its utmost pitch. In a window-seat of the room lay a number of chisels and other carpenter's tools. I know not what infatuation instantaneously seized me. The idea was too powerful to be resisted. . . . I snatched a tool suitable for the purpose, threw myself upon the ground, and applied with eagerness to a magazine which inclosed all for which my heart panted. After two or three efforts, in which the energy of uncontrollable passion was added to my bodily strength, the fastenings gave way, the trunk opened, and all that I sought was at once within my reach. I was in the act of lifting up the lid, when Mr. Falkland entered, wild, breathless, distracted in his looks! . . . He no sooner saw me, than his eyes emitted sparks of rage. He ran with eagerness to a brace of loaded pistols which hung in the room, and seizing one, presented it to my head. . . . but with the same rapidity with which he had formed his resolution, he changed it, and instantly went to the window, and flung the pistol into the court below. . . . The reader can with difficulty form a conception of the state to which I was now reduced. My act was in some sort an act of insanity; but how undescribable are the feelings with which I looked back upon it! It was an instantaneous impulse, a short-lived and passing alienation of mind; but what must Mr. Falkland think of that alienation? . . . My offence had merely been a mistaken thirst of knowledge. Such however it was, as to admit neither of forgiveness nor remission. This epoch was the crisis of my fate, dividing what may be called the offensive part from the defensive, which was the sole business of my remaining years. (*CW*, pp. 152–54)

Accident again plays an important part in the events of this encounter. Caleb "accidentally" goes into Falkland's apartment in volume 1, he is accidentally ("by some mysterious fatality") directed to Falkland's apartment here in volume 2, and Falkland accidentally appears in the apartment in time to prevent Caleb from observing the contents—if, in fact, there are any—of the trunk. Once again, the reader's attention is directed away from the overt to the implicit, from the external event to the implied processes behind the event. There is a force clearly larger than the characters themselves which impels them into activity. Such a force Caleb refers to as a "passing alienation of mind," as if to suggest that his actions may be measured against some unnamed rational norm of behavior and thereby be classified as deviant or aberrant. But the fact that the norm, or what Godwin might call the "moral," is unnamed suggests that this is a passage preoccupied with tendency, with the psychological effects of mind rather than the ethical categories of reason. The passage reads like psychodrama, with the characters acting out their latent fears and desires. Caleb calls his own activity "a mistaken thirst for knowledge," but he only calls it "mistaken" after he has been discovered. Similarly, Falkland regards Caleb's actions as a threatening violation of his privacy and is prepared to kill his tormentor, and yet relents, realizing, evidently, that killing him will not put a stop to what he is doing.

What is extremely peculiar, but psychologically suggestive, about this passage is that Caleb and Falkland do not speak to one another. Their actions defy discourse; their strength of feeling defies description. The effect of this absence of discourse is to drive the reader inward, to a form of participation in what is apparently unnameable. The scene, to use Caleb's phrase, is "too powerful to be resisted," just as Caleb and Falkland find one another too powerful to be resisted. This all suggests that what Caleb most desires is to become an active participant in Falkland's mind, to share his guilt and fear, and to act them out so violently that Falkland will have to accept him as a psychological accomplice. Caleb wishes to reenact Falkland's torment, not merely to discover and experience the other's feelings, but to raise himself—

at least psychologically, if not socially and politically—to the level of Falkland's coequal. The epoch of mind, to which Godwin earlier referred, represents Caleb's attempt to appropriate Falkland to his own consciousness, and to possess Falkland's experiences as if they were his own. Caleb speaks of his own offense as admitting "neither of forgiveness nor remission," which is a precise equivalent to Falkland's estimation of the consequences of his murder of Tyrrel. Caleb further asserts that this "epoch was the crisis of my fate," but it is well to see that it is also the crisis of Falkland's fate. Similarly, Caleb speaks of the scene as "dividing what may be called the offensive part from the defensive, which was the sole business of my remaining years," but this sentence applies with equal force to Falkland. He, like Caleb, is on the defensive for the remainder of the novel. Thus what occurs to both Falkland and Caleb is that they imprison one another within their own consciousness, and they alternately escape and pursue one another throughout the remainder of the novel.

By attaching a shared language of psychological complicity to both characters, Godwin circumvents the possibility of his novel becoming a kind of melodrama, with one character the hero and the other the villain. Instead, we have a form of psychological doubling, where each character becomes a part of the other's mind, and the doubling will culminate with Caleb's desire to identify himself fully with Falkland's experiences. In fact, what immediately follows this scene is that Falkland confesses to Caleb that he is the murderer of Tyrrel, that he is responsible for the mistaken execution of the Hawkinses for that murder, and that because of this confession Caleb must swear an oath as his accomplice. As Falkland says, "I had no alternative but to make you my confidant or my victim. . . . My tongue has now for the first time for several years spoken the language of my heart" (*CW*, p. 157). The result of this bond is, according to Caleb, that "I had made myself a prisoner, in the most intolerable sense of that term, for years—perhaps for the rest of my life" (*CW*, p. 159). But the act of imprisonment is as much desired as feared; for it means that Caleb has become a permanent part of Falkland's mind, it means that he can more fully experience Falkland's psychological agony, it means that the novel's basic language is now "the language of the heart," and it means that Caleb, who is as much as a prisoner of Falkland's consciousness, has now moved several steps closer to the discovery, or so he hopes, of the contents of Falkland's trunk.

Caleb's third and final mentioning of the trunk is precipitated by his discovery that Falkland has been circulating a narrative about him which eventually drives him out of his idyllic retreat in Wales. The narrative, designed to prove Caleb's criminality, is entitled "Wonderful and Surprising History of Caleb Williams" (*CW*, p. 349); and in response to this narrative Caleb "began to write [his own story] soon after" (*CW*, p. 351). I have mentioned before how Caleb and Falkland are imprisoned within each other's consciousness, and now their mutual complicity permits us to view them, literally, as vying authors, each attempting to write the nature of the other's existence and experiences. What this experience of vying authorship accomplishes within the reader is a dissolution of rational detachment; affective tendency supplants abstract moral. There is no adequate way to assess Caleb or Falkland either externally or independently, for psychologically they are processes of the same epoch of mind. They are attempting to write each other's story, but theirs is a single story of mutual disclosure and concealment. For both characters, as we can see in the following passage, the trunk is simultaneously an object of projection and entrapment:

Falkland! art thou the offspring in whom the lineaments of these tyrants are faithfully preserved? Was the world, with all its climates, made in vain for thy helpless, unoffending victim? Tremble! Tyrants have trembled surrounded with whole armies of their Janissaries! What should make thee inaccessible to my fury? No, I will use no daggers! I will unfold a tale—! I will show thee to the world for what thou art; and all the men that live shall confess my truth! . . . I will tell a tale—! The justice of the country shall hear me! the elements of nature in universal uproar shall not interrupt me! I will speak with a voice more fearful than thunder! . . . This is a moment pregnant with fate. I know—I think I know—that I will be triumphant, and crush my seemingly omnipotent foe. . . . With this little pen I defeat all his machinations; I stab him in the very point he was most solicitous to defend! . . . The pen lingers in my trembling fingers! Is there anything I have left unsaid?—The contents of the fatal trunk, from which all my misfortunes originated, I have never been able to ascertain. I once thought it contained some murderous instrument or relic, connected with the fate of the unhappy Tyrrel. I am now persuaded that the secret it incloses, is a faithful narrative of that and its concomitant transactions, written by Mr. Falkland, and reserved in case of the worst, that if by any unforeseen event his guilt should come to be fully disclosed, it might contribute to redeem the wreck of his reputation. But the truth or the falsehood of this conjecture is of little moment. If Falkland shall never be detected to the satisfaction of the world, such narrative will probably never see the light. In that case this story of mine may amply, severely perhaps, supply its place (*CW*, pp. 364–66).

If a tendency is revealed in this passage it is Caleb's desire to replace Falkland by a process of reenactment. He will substitute his narrative for what he believes may be a "faithful narrative" enclosed in Falkland's trunk, and thus he will raise to consciousnes what Falkland wishes to conceal. But substitution is not Caleb's only motive; he will reenact Falkland's crime, not purely as a matter of narrative description, with Caleb as an outside observer looking in. No: he will do to Falkland with words what Falkland did to Tyrrel with a knife. The process of reenactment has led Caleb to a form of murder. He says he will "use no daggers," but his tale is a weapon used to "crush my seemingly omnipotent foe"—"crush" being a word normally assigned to Falkland's vocabulary (i.e., p. 177). More important, the tale will "*stab* [my italics] him in the very point he was most solicitous to defend." Caleb's final attempt to take possession of Falkland's mind, his final attempt to fill the trunk with meaning, is to write a narrative, based on the projected contents of Falkland's suspected narrative hidden in the trunk, to "supply its place." But Caleb's apparent desire to get out the truth is, in fact, a confession both of his own culpability and of the limitations of his commitment to the power of purely rational description.

One section in this passage, especially, shortcircuits the possibility of construing all this as melodrama, with Falkland the vicious oppressor and Caleb his unwitting victim. It is the section referring to Falkland: "I will unfold a tale—! I will show thee to the world for what thou art; and all men that shall live shall confess my truth!" There is a striking approach-avoidance quality to these sentences, where Caleb alternates between the very familiar use of "thee" and "thou," suggesting an intimate relationship, and then pulls away with "my truth." The whole passage, in fact, alternates between questions, suggesting uncertainty, and bold declarations enforcing the idea of absolute conviction. The effect on the reader is to make us waver between political melodrama and psychological obsession. We are lured by the former only to be plunged into the latter. Caleb and the reader have got in more deeply than they realized or consciously desired. What they have got into is the convolution of mind rather than the expected revolution in society. Caleb wants Falkland to appear a tyrant and murderer, and by social standards of equity and justice Falkland certainly is these things. But psychologically Caleb is as much a tyrant and murderer as Falkland is socially, and a case might be made that Caleb is here tyrannizing the reader with his "truth." Caleb wishes to destroy Falkland not because he is a murderer but because, voluntarily or involuntarily, he has taken possession of Caleb's mind. But in order to destroy Falkland by revealing his secret, Caleb must reveal more of himself than he intends or would find desirable. He expects to show Falkland for what he is, so that men "shall confess my truth"—suggesting that the two are separable—but if there is truth to be found it can only be discovered so long as the reader refuses to separate the one character from the other.

Much has recently been made of the fact that Godwin wrote, and then rejected, an alternate conclusion to the one we presently possess. One critic has argued that the present conclusion, in effect, falsifies the novel, but I see it as enhancing the psychological tendency and affective appeal and rightly minimizing the overt political theme of injustice.[5] The original (or alternate) conclusion keeps the novel on the level of political melodrama, with Caleb as victim, and with the reader left hearing only Caleb's "truth." Falkland has not publicly confessed, Caleb is imprisoned, and there is a strong implication that he has been drugged by Falkland's agents. The effect of this conclusion is to see Caleb as the monumental victim of injustice, complete with gravestone ("HERE LIES WHAT WAS ONCE A MAN!"):[6]

I understand that Mr. Falkland contrary to all previous appearance still lives, nay, that he is considerably better in his health. Alas! Alas! it too plainly appears in my history that persecution and tyranny can never die! . . . There was once a poor traveller—he was very good natured—and very innocent—and meant no ill to any living soul—he met with a wild beast—the creature seemed to be in great distress, and moaned most piteously—I forget whether it had hurt itself—but the traveller came up to it, and asked it what it wanted, and would have assisted it—but the cries of the beast were only an imposition! —It was a CROCODILE! (*Appendix*, 332–33)

Everything in this passage is explicit, dichotomous, and melodramatic: the innocent soul, Caleb, has been conquered by the arch-villain, Falkland. The charitable traveler has been mauled by a vicious beast. But this conclusion, as Godwin evidently realized, simply does not mesh with the novel's tendency. Perhaps this is the sort of scene Godwin originally intended, for we know that he wrote the three volumes of the novel in reverse order (*CW*, p. xxv). But by the time he had read or written his way through volumes 2 and 1 back to volume three he may have realized that the novel had changed direction from its original political intent. We also know that Godwin ran into considerable trouble writing volume 3—he was stalled for three months (*CW*, p. xxx)—and this, coupled with the rejection of the original conclusion, suggests that the psychological tendency of the first two volumes simply did not correspond to the intended political moral of the third.

In the present conclusion, however, Falkland does publicly confess, Caleb is not imprisoned, and the interests of the political moral are subordinated to the larger claims of psychological tendency:

"Williams," said he [Falkland], "you have conquered! I see too late the greatness and elevation of your mind. I confess that it is to my fault and not yours, that it is to the excess of jealousy that was ever burning in my bosom, that I owe my ruin. I could have resisted any plan of malicious accusation you might have brought against me. But I see that the artless and manly story you have told, has carried conviction to every hearer. All my prospects are concluded. . . . I stand now completely detected. . . ." He survived this dreadful scene but three days. I have been his murderer. . . . It would have been merciful in comparison if I had planted a dagger in his heart. . . . Why should my reflections perpetually centre upon myself?—self, an overweening regard to which has been the source of my errors! Falkland, I will think only of thee, and from that thought will draw ever-fresh nourishment for my sorrows!. . . . I began these memoirs with the idea of vindicating my character. I have now no character that I wish to vindicate: but I will finish them that thy story may be fully understood, and that if those errors of thy life be known, which thou so ardently desiredst to conceal, the world may at least not hear and repeat a half-told and mangled tale. (*CW*, pp. 376–78)

The first part of this section, where Falkland publicly confesses, could have maintained the sense of political melodrama, with Falkland, the oppressor, confessing his injustice to Caleb. But the second part of the passage undermines the political moral, for Falkland's confession clearly does not satisfy Caleb, nor is it allowed to satisfy the reader. Although the reader is lured repeatedly throughout the novel into believing that a public confession will provide a satisfactory resolution, based on the rational establishment of truth, it multiplies complexity rather than reduces it. Falkland becomes an object of sympathy, and so does Caleb. Falkland may believe himself to stand "completely detected," but he is not, nor is Caleb. What the final scene repeatedly emphasizes is a sense of mutual complicity, where the desire to detect and confess strongly accentuates not the expected rational illumination but psychological frustration. The reader is led to a sense of psychological truth larger than any political intent. Both characters are simultaneously vindicated and vanquished. As two apparently separate men, they have lived out one story, or one epoch of mind. They are antagonists—politically, socially, and psychologically—but their conflict is one of parallel lines which, paradoxically, intersect. Their apparent opposition culminates in a process of mutual identification.

Falkland, for example, says that Caleb's "artless and manly story . . . has carried conviction to every hearer," but I daresay that Falkland's confession, as well, carries a similar amount of conviction with the reader. Falkland says his "prospects are concluded," but Caleb believes his own "prospects" to be concluded. Falkland confesses that he is a murderer, but Caleb believes himself to be one, and he is—at least psychologically. The dagger is mentioned to reinforce their murderous sense of identity. Falkland and Caleb are both preoccupied with vindicating their characters, and now neither man believes himself to have a character worth vindicating. Just as important, Caleb and Falkland, and, I believe, the reader as well, are led to ponder the question, prompted throughout the novel by external events: "Why should my reflection perpetually centre upon myself?" There is no explicit answer to this question, but the last words of the novel imply a direction, if not an ultimate destination: so that "the world may at least not hear and repeat a half-told and mangled tale."

The "half-told and mangled tale" would emerge if in reading *Caleb Williams* the reader were to adopt, exclusively, either Caleb's or Falkland's point of view. Such a procedure, which is represented by the original (but rejected) conclusion of the novel, would distort the reader's experience of the novel by focusing on abstract moral at the expense of psychological tendency, observation at the expense of participation. Such melodramatic readings are evident in recent criticism. James Boulton and David McCracken view the novel politically, with Falkland emerging as the victim of his own obsessive commitment to the principles of chivalry and aristocracy. D. Gilbert Dumas voices strong reservations about the novel's conclusion because "Truth, that is, innocence [by which Dumas means Caleb] triumphs by default, not by its own strength," and he further argues, sustaining a melodramatic reading, that "in exchanging his role of political philosopher and propagandist for that of ethical exhorter, Godwin becomes guilty in the novel of contradictions in doctrine and style similar to those in the first edition of *Political Justice*."[7] But what appear to be contradictions, in strictly rational terms, are encompassed by the novel's much larger psychological interests.

I have concentrated on how one central object—the trunk—encloses and unfolds the psychological tendency of the novel. The trunk acts as a lure and a source of illumination both for the reader and for Caleb, who acts as a participant in, and agent of, curiosity. When I say "illumination" I do so paradoxically: strictly speaking, there is nothing discovered within the trunk, but the trunk serves as an occasion for eliciting and stimulating the reader's own psychological awareness. The trunk is an analogue to the novel's narrative process; it does not, in Godwin's terms, contain a moral so much as it is an embodiment of psychological tendency. The interesting critical question, then, is How does one rationally describe the meaning of *Caleb Williams* in such a way as to account for the affective appeal of the novel's psychological tendency?

Here I would take my cue from two critics, William Hazlitt and Rudolf Storch. What Hazlitt says about the *Enquiry Concerning Political Justice* applies, as well, to *Caleb Williams:*

If it is admitted that Reason alone is not the sole and self-sufficient ground of morals, it is to Mr. Godwin that we are indebted for having settled the point. No one denied or distrusted this principle (before his time) as the absolute judge and interpreter in all questions of difficulty; and if this is no longer the case, it is because he has taken this principle, and followed it into its remotest consequences with more keenness of eye and steadiness of hand than any other expounder of ethics. His grand work is (at least) an *experimentum crucis* to show the weak sides and imperfections of human reason as the sole law of human action.[8]

How Hazlitt's observations may be applied to the novel can be seen in Rudolf Storch's essentially psychological approach to *Caleb Williams:*

In *Caleb Williams* the conflict between rebellion and guilt remains unresolved.
. . . The remarkable thing about *Caleb Williams* is that it shows life to be completely irrational. . . . the two characters [Caleb and Falkland] are not separate
and interacting, but aspects of one and the same soul, so that their conflicts
and the fate that binds them together have indeed the force of inescapable
destiny. . . . Falkland, Tyrrel, Caleb and Clare are not so much separate persons with their own motivations (or characters in an observed society) as elements within the mind of one person who projects them warring one against
the other onto the figures moving in this strange dreamlike story.[9]

Such readings certainly conform with Godwin's comment on the
composition of *Caleb Williams:* "The thing in which my imagination
revelled the most freely, was the analysis of the private and internal
operations of the mind" (*CW*, p. xxviii), and with his further assertions:
"Human affairs are so entangled, motives are so subtle and variously
compounded, that the truth cannot be told" (*ENQ*, pp. 288–89), and
"The mere external actions of man are not worth the studying: Who
would have ever thought of going through a course of history, if the
science were comprised in a set of chronological tables? No: it is the
hearts of men we should study. It is to their actions, as expressive of
disposition and character, we should attend." [10]

What all these comments suggest is that the structure of *Caleb
Williams* is not progressive, but obsessive, cyclical, and recapitulatory.
The events of the novel are primarily the occasion for psychological
inquiry.[11] Every trial in the narrative is not just an external event, point-
int toward a specified moral or rational solution, but rather a vehicle
for internal psychological examination whereby the reader, like Caleb,
not only observes but participates within the dynamics of the novel's
tendency. The novel thus becomes an epoch in the mind of the reader,
in which the reader is led to abandon the idea that "reason alone is . . .
the sole and self-sufficient ground of morals." Beginning as an observer who is both confident of, and expects to describe, the truth, the
reader, like Caleb, becomes entangled in the experience of psychological truth—in what Godwin calls "the hearts of men." This inward
tendency which drives the reader away from politics and society into
psychology and the processes of mind, away from the abstractions of
reason to an affective appeal to the human heart, stands as Godwin's
supreme response to the idea of the impossible observer.

9
Criticism and the Idea of Nature

It was Samuel Johnson who made the provocative statement that "there is always an appeal open from criticism to nature" (*Shakespeare*, 7:67). The matter of precisely defining the concept, or concepts, of nature in the eighteenth century is, as Arthur Lovejoy has memorably demonstrated, a very tricky problem.[1] However, my interests are determined less by the exact meaning of the term than by the significance of the gesture, especially as it illumines the diverse views of human nature in the texts I have considered. Concepts of nature are often tacit assumptions, as we have seen in the way that Swift and Mandeville use reason or in Richardson's and Fielding's differing responses to the "state of probation." But these are also the very assumptions that allow authors, readers, and critics to proceed in their own activities with a sense, however problematical, of common understanding.

Johnson's criticism is exemplary in this respect, for it reveals how the appeal to nature can determine both the strengths and limitations of any critical approach. Thus when he repeatedly reaffirms that "nothing can please many and please long, but just representations of general nature" (*Shakespeare*, 7:61), that Shakespeare is above all writers "the poet of nature" who "always makes nature predominate over accident" (*Shakespeare*, 7:62, 65), and that his plays exhibit "the real state of sublunary nature" (*Shakespeare*, 7:66), he is confident that we, like Johnson, at least tacitly know and are responsive to the experience of nature to which he appeals. However, like customs, ideas of nature may and do change, though more slowly than customs; and as they change so do the possibilities of meaning.[2] Thus when Johnson remarks on the oddity of *Tristram Shandy*, commenting that nothing odd will last—a view, by the way, that he shares

with Richardson—his observation demonstrates that he as a reader and
critic has reached a point where his idea of nature cannot accommodate
the experience proposed by a particular literary text.[3] As we have seen
earlier, the same thing happens when Johnson reads *Paradise Lost*.
Because *Paradise Lost*, in his view, "comprises neither human actions
nor human manners"—both determined by Johnson's idea of nature—
he argues that the reader "finds no transaction in which he can be
engaged." Johnson's idea of nature, then, does not refer to external
nature, but to his own sense of human nature as the affective basis
of literary meaning.

The boundaries of Johnson's idea of nature may be generally defined
by sacred verse on the one hand and the oddity of *Tristram Shandy* on
the other. Though Johnson recognizes the "Theocracy" as a vital part of
human history, he no longer regards it as a live part—that is, within
the imaginative literary experience—of the literary audience of the
eighteenth century. This assumption is so strong that the very term
"sacred poetry" involves a process of mutual exclusion; for, as Johnson
declares in the *Life of Waller*, "Contemplative piety, or the intercourse
between God and the human soul, cannot be poetical. Man admitted
to implore the mercy of his Creator and plead the merits of his Redeemer is already in a higher state than poetry can confer" (*Lives*,
1:291). Such a conviction may explain why Johnson has more to say
about the moral and psychological impact of *Clarissa* than about its
Christian meaning. Even so, Johnson is clearly aware that his own limitations are conditioned by his idea of nature, and his criticism demonstrates how such limitations necessarily influence his experience of
reading and his practice of criticism. If, as Johnson said, "Imitations
produce pain or pleasure, not because they are mistaken for realities,
but because they bring realities to mind" (*Shakespeare*, 7:78), it obviously follows that what he cannot imaginatively reenact cannot bring
realities to mind and thus cannot have an affective appeal.

In this regard, Johnson's comments about the reader's ability to
participate in literature, and how this ability is ultimately tied to an idea
of nature, anticipate R. G. Collingwood's doctrine of historical thought
and the idea of history:

Historical knowledge is the knowledge of what mind has done in the past, and
at the same time it is the redoing of this, the perpetuation of past acts in the

present. Its object is therefore not a mere object, something outside the mind which knows it; it is an activity of thought, which can be known only in so far as the knowing mind reenacts it and knows itself as so doing. To the historian, the activities whose history he is studying are not spectacles to be watched, but experiences to be lived through in his own mind; they are objective, or known to him, only because they are also subjective, or activities of his own.

It may thus be said that historical inquiry reveals to the historian the powers of his own mind. Since all he can know historically is thoughts that he can rethink for himself, the fact of his coming to know them shows him that his mind is able (or by the very effort of studying them has become able) to think in these ways. And conversely, whenever he finds certain historical matters unintelligible, he has discovered a limitation of his own mind; he has discovered that there are certain ways in which he is not, or no longer, or not yet, able to think.[4]

The key idea in Collingwood's formulation is that the experiences reenacted are both objective and subjective—that, in fact, only experiences which we can subjectively re-create, either through reason or imagination, can become meaningful for us. Indeed, Collingwood's distinction between "spectacles to be watched" and "experiences to be lived through" closely approximates my distinction between observation and participation and parallels Johnson's dismissal of what I call the impossible observer. The ideal reader, like the ideal historian, is one who, not exclusively dependent on abstract observation, has the imaginative ability to apprehend the motions and experiences of other minds. But it should also be evident that the reader's apprehension of meaning is largely determined by his idea of nature (or human nature), which operates as a conscious or unconscious assumption both prior to and during the experience of reading and the act of criticism. Furthermore, since the idea of nature is so frequently a tacit assumption, it is entirely possible that when we consider literary texts from the past— perhaps even from the present—we may have difficulty determining the idea of nature informing a particular act of composition, not to say an entire literary tradition.

What makes our understanding of literature even more complicated is that, while the idea of nature is often tacit, it is also often in a state of flux. This was particularly true in the eighteenth century, for, as Melvyn New has persuasively argued:

A proper "conceptual context" for Defoe and Richardson, Fielding and Smollett, must embody not only the providential design, but also what was happening to that design in the course of the century and in different hands. That is to say, the major novelists of the age imaged forth in their writings neither the Christian world view, which was slowly giving way, nor the secular world view, which we now recognize as having replaced it; rather . . . their fictions reflect . . . that historical moment when the intellectual and imaginative resources of their culture were transferred from one system of ordering experience to another. The proper frame of reference, then, for the great English fictions of the eighteenth century is one that defines this transition.[5]

The crucial word is transition, and I believe New can document this transition because, for one thing, he considers individual texts without presuming larger generalizations about an author's entire corpus. In other words, instead of assuming that all of Defoe's works enact a similar spiritual meaning, it is safer to say, as I have argued, that spiritual meaning is clearly evident in *Robinson Crusoe*, but much less so in *Moll Flanders* and *Roxana*. Indeed, the very transition between spiritual and secular views appears to occur within Defoe's fiction. The same thing might be said for Fielding's fiction, where providential design predominates in *Tom Jones*, but is far more problematical in *Amelia*. In the case of *Clarissa* one might argue that the novel powerfully dramatizes the transition between Clarissa's religious convictions and the secular assumptions of the majority of characters in the novel, as well as of a good many readers. It is not until *Caleb Williams* that the transition from spiritual to secular meaning is complete.

Moreover, the presence of this transition between secular and religious orders of experience may help us to understand not only why the critical views of eighteenth-century literature differ so widely, but why the individual works I have discussed are so problematical. They are problematical because, in diverse ways, they straddle different ideas of nature which are in the process of transition. By examining a broad range of works that address themselves to what I have called the impossible observer, I have attempted to take into account the transition in the eighteenth-century idea of nature and the author's manipulation of this change in order to question the reader's traditional assumptions concerning human nature. All these works, I have argued, construct their affective appeal by at once anticipating the reader's habits of detached contemplation and creating occasions that are calculated to encourage or enforce a more intimate, and sometimes less determinate, participation with the text. Inevitably the affective impact of such participation takes different forms; but in every case the authors challenge the reader's uninspected exercise of, and dependence on, reason.

On the other hand, some of the most familiar and influential approaches to eighteenth-century literature presume the stability of reason and the adequacy of detached observation. This faith in a tradition of order, reason, and stability is eloquently expressed in the preface of Martin Battestin's *The Providence of Wit:*

The poetry of Pope and Gay, the fiction of Fielding and Goldsmith, the music and building and gardens of the period—all, in various ways, attest to the faith of the age in Order, to the conviction that Art is the attribute of Reality. . . . that some at least of the salient formal features of Augustan literature and the arts—balance and proportion and design, for example, whether conceived geometrically or as a movement through time toward some pre-determined ending—are best understood in terms of the ontological assumptions of the Christian humanist tradition.[6]

Now it would be foolish to argue that no such tradition exists in the eighteenth century, but there are many eighteenth-century works, such as those I have examined, which do not satisfy such expectations of balance, proportion, and design. Battestin himself concedes this point when he refers to his last chapter on Swift and Sterne as a "negative demonstration" (p. ix) of his argument; he is quite aware that the confident use of art and artifice in many of the works of Pope, Fielding, Gay, and Goldsmith may not apply to other eighteenth-century writers.

In a sense, therefore, my book is a positive demonstration of an eighteenth-century tradition of literature which is different from, but exists along side of, the providential tradition that Battestin discusses. Briefly put, the tradition that Battestin examines tends to situate the reader in the position of an observer, and continually appeals to the reader's reason, reinforcing his expectations of order, because there is within this tradition a strong underlying assurance of providential design. However, the tradition I have discussed elicits the reader's active participation with the text, and it appeals beyond his reliance on reason to a less determinate, but no less vital, awareness of the problematical aspects of human reason. Battestin speaks of "a movement through time toward some pre-determined ending," whereas I have concentrated on works whose endings are less predetermined and providential than they are problematical. Even *Clarissa*, whose Christian meaning would seem to accord with Battestin's providential tradition, presents itself as a highly problematical novel because of Richardson's strong views about this life as a "state of probation."

What is especially fascinating about these two traditions and their diverse appeals to nature is that they appear to require different methods of reading and thus different modes of criticism. For example, Battestin focuses on how the presence of balance, proportion, and design "are best understood in terms of the ontological assumptions of the Christian humanist tradition." Yet these same properties of art are the subject of Eric Rothstein's *Systems of Order and Inquiry in Later Eighteenth-Century Fiction*, but he does not find the same idea of nature, if you will, that Battestin does. Rothstein writes, "in all five novels [*Rasselas, Tristram Shandy, Humphry Clinker, Amelia, Caleb Williams*] form—pattern, design, order—is keyed to a concern with epistemological inquiry."[7] Thus we see two intelligent and responsible critics considering the same attributes of art (though not always the same texts), and arriving at wholly different ideas of nature: the one arguing for a predominantly religious meaning, while the other emphasizes a secular concern with epistemology.

Since both approaches are persuasive, we are clearly faced with a critical dilemma; but it may be a revelation in disguise. That is, I would say that this dilemma is, in fact, convincing evidence of two traditions of literature—call them providential and problematical—existing simultaneously in the eighteenth century. I see no reason why we have to choose one over the other.

Notes

Chapter 1

1. Lee Andrew Elioseff, *The Cultural Milieu of Addison's Literary Criticism* (Austin: University of Texas Press, 1963), p. 6.

2. Edmund Burke, *A Philosophical Enquiry into the Origin of Our Ideas of the Sublime and Beautiful*, ed. J. T. Boulton (London: Routledge and Kegan Paul, 1958), pp. 172, 175.

3. Sir Joshua Reynolds, *Discourses on Art*, intro. Robert R. Wark (London: Collier, 1969), p. 203.

4. The Yale Edition of the *Works of Samuel Johnson*, vols. 7 and 8, *Johnson on Shakespeare*, ed. Arthur Sherbo (New Haven, Conn.: Yale University Press, 1968), 7:67. Hereafter cited as *Shakespeare*.

5. Ibid., vol. 2, *The Idler and Adventurer*, ed. W. J. Bate et al. (New Haven, Conn.: Yale University Press, 1963), 2:493. Johnson later mentions "the movements of the human passions . . . of which every man carries the archetype within him" (2:496). Hereafter cited as *Idler and Adventurer*.

6. Emerson R. Marks has suggested, "For all his [Johnson's] references to judging by principle and to the 'science' of criticism, he was profoundly skeptical of attempts to rationalize experience." At the same time, however, Marks's observation must be set within the context of his damning view that "no other critic before or since ever set out on his career burdened with convictions about literature more inimical on the whole to good criticism" (*The Poetics of Reason* [New York: Random House, 1968], pp. 116, 118. For an opposed and more compelling view of Johnson's criticism "as a way of reading," see Leopold Damrosch, Jr., *The Uses of Johnson's Criticism* (Charlottesville: University of Virginia Press, 1976).

7. Richard Schlegel, "The Impossible Spectator in Physics," *Centennial Review* 19 (Fall 1975): 217–31.

8. *Eighteenth-Century Studies* 9 (Spring 1976): 307–32; quotation, p. 331.

9. I am here borrowing from Paul Alper's definition of mode as "man's strength relative to his world." See "Mode in Narrative Poetry," in *To Tell a Story: Narrative Theory and Practice* (Los Angeles: William Andrews Clark Memorial Library, 1973), p. 31.

10. See the following works by Iser: "Indeterminacy and the Reader's Response in Prose Fiction," in *Aspects of Narrative*, ed. J. Hillis Miller (New York: Columbia University Press, 1971), pp. 1–45; "The Reading

Process: A Phenomenological Approach," *New Literary History* 3 (Winter 1972): 279–99; "The Reality of Fiction: A Functionalist Approach to Literature," *New Literary History* 7 (Autumn 1975): 7–38; *The Implied Reader* (Baltimore, Md.: Johns Hopkins University Press, 1973).

11. *Boswell's Life of Johnson*, ed. George Birkbeck Hill, rev. L. F. Powell, 6 vols. (Oxford: Clarendon Press, 1934–50), 2:48–49. Hereafter cited as *Life*. See also Arthur Sherbo's useful essay, "'Characters of Manners': Notes toward the History of a Critical Term," *Criticism* 11 (Fall 1969): 343–57.

12. Joseph Epes Brown, *The Critical Opinions of Samuel Johnson* (New York: Russel & Russel, 1961), p. 347.

13. *Selected Letters of Samuel Richardson*, ed. John Carroll (Oxford: Clarendon Press, 1964), p. 108. Hereafter cited as *Selected Letters*.

Chapter 2

1. See Ernest Tuveson, ed., *Swift: A Collection of Critical Essays* (Englewood Cliffs, N.J.: Prentice-Hall, 1964), pp. 15–29.

2. *The Correspondence of Alexander Pope*, ed. George Sherburn, 5 vols. (Oxford: Clarendon Press, 1956), 3:366.

3. See Edward W. Rosenheim, Jr., *Swift and the Satirist's Art* (Chicago: University of Chicago Press, 1963), pp. 12–18, 109–12.

4. For instance, the reason and moderation that Swift recommends in such nonsatirical works as *The Contests and Dissensions in Athens and Rome* and *The Sentiments of a Church-of-England Man* do not, in my view, emerge as forceful "positives" in *A Tale of a Tub* or *Gulliver's Travels*. This is not surprising in *Gulliver's Travels*, because Swift knew he was attacking the definition of man as *animal rationale*. See *The Correspondence of Jonathan Swift*, ed. Harold Williams, 5 vols. (Oxford: Clarendon Press, 1963–65), 3:103, 118. Hereafter cited as *Correspondence*.

5. *The Prose Works of Jonathan Swift*, ed. Herbert Davis, 14 vols. (Oxford: Blackwell, 1939–68), 1:107–10. All volume and page references to Swift's works will be to this edition.

6. On the other hand, Rosenheim has argued that the two famous paragraphs on madness are among the few sources "of whatever fundamental beliefs with respect to morality and metaphysics we can attribute to Swift" (*Swift and the Satirist's Art*, p. 198).

7. P. K. Elkin, *The Augustan Defence of Satire* (Oxford: Clarendon Press, 1973), p. 9.

8. The relationship of the reader to Swift's satires has been discussed from a variety of perspectives in the following recent essays: Claude J. Rawson, "Gulliver and the Gentle Reader," in *Imagined Worlds*, ed. Maynard Mack and Ian Gregor (London: Methuen, 1968), pp. 51–90; Gardner D. Stout, Jr., "Speaker and Satiric Vision in Swift's *Tale of a Tub*," *Eighteenth-Century Studies* 3 (Winter 1969): 175–99; W. B. Carnochan, "Swift's *Tale*: On Satire, Negation, and The Uses of Irony," *Eighteenth-Century Studies* 5 (Fall 1971): 122–44; John N. Morris, "Wishes as Horses: A Word for the Houyhnhnms," *Yale Review* 62 (Spring 1973): 372–91. The critic to whom I am most indebted

is Stanley E. Fish, particularly his liberating essay, "Literature in the Reader: Affective Stylistics," first published in *New Literary History* 2 (Autumn 1970): 123–62, and most of it reprinted in *Self-Consuming Artifacts* (Berkeley and Los Angeles: University of California Press, 1972).

9. *Swift and the Satirist's Art*, p. 31.

10. See especially R. C. Elliott's fine essay, "Swift's 'I,'" *Yale Review* 62 (Spring 1973): 372–91.

11. With respect to Ireland, for example, see Swift's bitter remarks concerning such distinctions in *An Answer to a Paper Called a Memorial*: "A fair Issue of Things, begun upon Party Rage, while some sacrificed the Publick to Fury, and others to Ambition! While a Spirit of Faction and Oppression reigned in every Part of the Country: where Gentlemen, instead of consulting the Ease of their Tenants, or cultivating their Lands, were worrying one another, upon Points of *Whig* and *Tory*, of *High Church* and *Low Church;* which no more concerned them, than the long and famous Controversy of *Strops for Razors*" (12:22–23).

12. *Correspondence*, 3:103.

Chapter 3

1. Bernard Mandeville, *Free Thoughts on Religion, the Church, and National Happiness* (London: T. Jauncy and J. Roberts, 1720), p. 81. Some of the language of my opening paragraph is taken from my review of two books on Mandeville—Richard I. Cook, *Bernard Mandeville* (New York: Twayne, 1974), and Hector Monroe, *The Ambivalence of Bernard Mandeville* (Oxford: Clarendon Press, 1975)—in *Eighteenth-Century Studies* 9 (Spring 1976): 457–59.

2. *The Fable of the Bees*, ed. F. B. Kaye, 2 vols. (Oxford: Clarendon Press, 1924), 1:405. This chapter, it should be noted, deals exclusively with part 1 of *The Fable*.

3. Here I am in agreement with Phillip Harth who, in his introduction to *The Fable of the Bees* (New York: Pelican Books, 1970), has argued that "Mandeville's remarkable talent as a satirist emerges as fully in the prose remarks and essays as in the little poem at the beginning of *The Fable of the Bees*. They show him turning from verse to prose, not in order to abandon satire, but to exploit it with greater freedom" (p. 40).

4. See Robert Adolph's essay, "Style, Satire, and Paradox," in *Mandeville Studies*, ed. Irwin Primer (Martinus Nijhoff: The Hague, 1975), pp. 159–61. This entire collection of essays—hereafter cited as *Mandeville Studies* —should prove indispensable to all future studies of Mandeville.

5. See, for example, Martin Price's remark in *To the Palace of Wisdom* (Garden City, N.Y.: Anchor Books, 1965), that "Mandeville's *Fable*, like Swift's account of the Yahoos, is an ironic attempt to show how much of human complexity *can* be reduced to a few low principles of compulsion" (p. 116). See also Thomas R. Edwards, "Mandeville's Moral Prose," *ELH* 31 (1964): "My view, in short, is that his irony, like Swift's, is based on a remarkable talent for parody, for giving dramatic embodiment to attitudes that are not, in any easy sense, his own" (p. 203).

6. *Mandeville Studies*, pp. 162–63.

7. My use of the term "manifest fiction," in relation to satire, is somewhat akin to Sheldon Sacks's definition of satire as "a work organized so that it ridicules objects external to the fictional world created in it" (*Fiction and the Shape of Belief* [Berkeley and Los Angeles: University of California Press, 1967], p. 26). With respect to Swift's use of the Houyhnhnms, for instance, I agree with Sacks that "the virtues ascribed to the Houyhnhnms have been chosen according to how well they facilitate the ridicule of certain of the traits, manners, and institutions of men" (p. 9).

8. *Mandeville Studies*, p. 176 (my italics).

9. I am thinking, for example, of the recent book by the anthropologist Colin Turnbull, *The Mountain People* (New York: Simon and Schuster, 1972), which could be read as the scientific verification of what for Swift was a manifest fiction—namely, the Yahoos. B. F. Skinner's *Beyond Freedom and Dignity* (New York: Bantam, 1971) is another work that examines latent assumptions. Because it is so strikingly similar to Mandeville's *Fable*, I will say more about Skinner's book later.

10. *Mandeville Studies*, p. 39.

11. See Irwin Primer's introduction to *The Fable of the Bees* (New York: Capricorn, 1962): "Much of the strength of Mandeville's argument lies in the fact that he repeatedly claims to be dealing with the facts" (p. 9).

12. *Mandeville Studies*, pp. 174, 40.

13. I am here unable to accept Phillip Harth's suggestion that "what unifies the disparate elements of his [Mandeville's] book is the single-mindedness, not of his argument, but of his satirical purpose" ("The Satiric Purpose of *The Fable of the Bees*," *Eighteenth-Century Studies* 2 [Summer 1969]: 334). I think Mandeville's empirical arguments are more wide-ranging than, though not exclusive of, his satirical purpose.

14. See F. A. Hayek, "Dr. Bernard Mandeville," *Proceedings of the British Academy* 52 (1966): 125–41. Hayek writes: "It is difficult to remember now . . . how closely religion was not long ago still associated with the 'argument from design.' The discovery of an astounding order which no man had designed was for most men the chief evidence for the existence of a personal creator. In the moral and political sphere Mandeville and Hume did show that the sense of justice and probity on which the order in this sphere rested, was not originally implanted in man's mind but had, like that mind itself, grown in a process of gradual evolution which at least in principle we might learn to understand. The revulsion against this suggestion was quite as great as that caused more than a century later when it was shown that the marvels of the organism could no longer be adduced as proof of special design" (p. 141).

15. It should be remembered that I am here confining my discussion to part 1 of *The Fable of the Bees*. Elias J. Chiasson examines part 2 in considerable detail in his article, "Bernard Mandeville: A Reappraisal," *Philological Quarterly* (October 1970): 489–519. Chiasson argues that "Mandeville's major thrust, in spite of the pyrotechnics and tomfoolery, must be placed in the context of that perennial problem of determining the relationship which exists between reason and faith, nature and grace" (p. 519). This is a fair

enough abstract description of much of part 2, but Professor Chiasson mistaken-
ly downplays the rich effects of Mandeville's style when he refers to their
"pyrotechnics and tomfoolery." See also *Mandeville Studies*, pp. 41–42.

16. See Leland D. Peterson's article, "Swift's *Project*: A Religious and
Political Satire," *PMLA* 82 (March 1967): 54–63, and Phillip Harth's convincing rebuttal, "Swift's *Project*: Tract or Travesty?" *PMLA* 84 (March 1969):
336–43.

17. F. A. Hayek, in "Dr. Bernard Mandeville" (pp. 133–34), quotes Josiah
Tucker's version of "Private Vices, Publick Benefits" in *The Elements of
Commerce and Theory of Taxes* (1755), "that *universal* mover in human nature,
SELF-LOVE, may receive such a direction in this case (as in all others) as to
promote the public interest by those efforts it shall make towards pursuing its
own."

18. See Primer's observation, "[Mandeville's] views on human psychology
consist mainly in specific analyses of pride, shame, fear, envy, jealousy,
avarice, prodigality, ambition, courage and other passions. Such cataloguing
and description in Mandeville seem to follow lines set down by Montaigne,
Hobbes, Locke, Bayle and La Rochefoucauld, among others. What is new in
Mandeville, or at least singularly accented, is his sense of a slowly developing,
evolutionary psychology" (introduction, *The Fable of the Bees*, p. 10).

Chapter 4

1. Everett Zimmerman, *Defoe and the Novel* (Berkeley and Los Angeles:
University of California Press, 1975), p. 17.

2. John J. Richetti, *Defoe's Narratives* (Oxford: Clarendon Press, 1975),
p. 9.

3. G. A. Starr, *Defoe and Casuistry* (Princeton: Princeton University Press,
1971), p. viii. See also the valuable appendix to Starr's book entitled "Fiction and Mendacity."

4. *The Letters of Daniel Defoe*, ed. George Harris Healey (Oxford: Clarendon Press, 1955), pp. 42–43. Hereafter cited as *Letters*. See also Maximillian E.
Novak's discussion of dissimulation in "Defoe's Use of Irony," *The Uses of
Irony* (Los Angeles: William Andrews Clark Memorial Library, 1966), pp.
7–38.

5. For another approach to Defoe's dissimulation, see Homer O. Brown,
"The Displaced Self in the Novels of Daniel Defoe," *ELH* 38 (1971): 562–90.
Brown argues, for example, that "Defoe's narrators seem under a double com-
pulsion to expose and to conceal themselves" (p. 563).

6. Virginia Woolf, *Collected Essays*, 4 vols. (London: Hogarth, 1966),
1:66. Hereafter cited as *CE*.

7. Charles Gildon, Preface to *The Life and Strange Surprizing Adventures
of Mr. D. . . . De F . . .* (1719), in the Norton edition of *Moll Flanders*,
ed. Edward Kelly (New York: Norton, 1973), pp. 324–25. Hereafter cited as
MF.

8. The works I am referring to are as follows: Maximillian E. Novak's
two books, *Economics and the Fiction of Daniel Defoe* (Berkeley and Los
Angeles: University of California Press, 1962), and *Defoe and the Nature of*

148 *Notes to Pages 51–71*

Man (Oxford: Clarendon Press, 1963); John Robert Moore, *Daniel Defoe: Citizen of the World* (Chicago: University of Chicago Press, 1958); G. A. Starr's two books, *Defoe and Spiritual Autobiography* (Princeton, N.J.: Princeton University Press, 1965), and *Defoe and Casuistry* (Princeton, N.J.: Princeton University Press, 1971); J. Paul Hunter, *The Reluctant Pilgrim* (Baltimore, Md.: Johns Hopkins University Press, 1966), and Ian Watt's two studies, "*Robinson Crusoe* as a Myth," in *Eighteenth-Century English Literature*, ed. James L. Clifford (New York: Oxford University Press, 1959), pp. 158–79, and *The Rise of the Novel* (Berkeley and Los Angeles: University of California Press, 1964), pp. 60–92.

9. By my count, forms of the term "deliverance" (including "deliver" and "delivered") appear in excess of fifty times in *Robinson Crusoe*.

10. *Robinson Crusoe*, ed. James Sutherland (Boston: Houghton Mifflin, 1968), p. 78. Hereafter cited as *RC*.

11. Brown, "Displaced Self," p. 589.

12. Allan McKillop makes a similar point in *The Early Masters of English Fiction* (Lawrence: University of Kansas Press, 1968), p. 30.

13. See Starr, *Defoe and Casuistry*, pp. 111–64.

14. Zimmerman, *Defoe and the Novel*, p. 5.

15. G. A. Starr, "Sympathy V. Judgement in Roxana's First Liaison," in *The Augustan Milieu*, ed. Henry Knight Miller, Eric Rothstein, and G. S. Rousseau (Oxford: Clarendon Press, 1970), pp. 59–76.

16. Ibid., p. 75.

17. Ibid., p. 71.

18. *Roxana*, ed. Jane Jack (London: Oxford University Press, 1968), p. 17. Hereafter cited as *R*.

19. Richetti argues that Roxana's "ultimate ambition lies in a powerful androgyny" (*Defoe's Narratives*, p. 195).

20. Michael Shinagel, *Daniel Defoe and Middle-Class Gentility* (Cambridge, Mass.: Harvard University Press, 1968), pp. 193–94.

21. Robert D. Hume, "The Conclusion of Defoe's *Roxana*: Fiasco or Tour de Force?" *Eighteenth-Century Studies* 3 (Summer 1970): 490; Everett Zimmerman, "Language and Character in Defoe's *Roxana*," *Essays in Criticism* 21 (1971): 234. Much of this essay is reprinted in his *Defoe and the Novel*; Maximillian E. Novak, "Crime and Punishment in Defoe's *Roxana*," *Journal of English and Germanic Philology* 65 (1966): 456. See also Wallace Jackson, "*Roxana* and The Development of Defoe's Fiction," *Studies in the Novel*, Summer 1975, 181–94.

22. David Leon Higdon, "The Critical Fortunes and Misfortunes of Defoe's *Roxana*," *Bucknell Review* 20 (Spring 1972): 74–75.

23. *Colonel Jack*, ed. Samuel Holt Monk (London: Oxford University Press, 1965), p. 163.

24. Richetti, *Defoe's Narratives*, p. 192.

Chapter 5

1. For further comments on this matter, see J. Paul Hunter, *Occasional Form* (Baltimore, Md.: Johns Hopkins University Press, 1975), pp. 212–14;

C. J. Rawson, *Henry Fielding and the Augustan Ideal under Stress* (London: Routledge & Kegan Paul, 1972), pp. 88–89, 95–96; Mark Kinkead-Weekes, *Samuel Richardson* (London: Methuen, 1973), pp. 468–72; and T. C. Duncan Eaves and Ben D. Kimpel, *Samuel Richardson* (Oxford: Clarendon Press, 1971), pp. 292–306.

2. *Selected Letters of Samuel Richardson*, ed. John Carroll (Oxford: Clarendon Press, 1964), p. 89. Hereafter cited as *SL*.

3. *Samuel Richardson, "Clarissa": Preface, Hints of Prefaces, and Postscript*, intro. R. F. Brissenden (Los Angeles: William Andrews Clark Memorial Library, 1964), pp. 1, 350–51. Hereafter cited as *PHP*. I should also note that although Brissenden has cautioned that "it is impossible to determine how much of *Hints of Prefaces* or of the published Preface or Postscript is Richardson's own work" (p. ii), it seems reasonable to assume, as I have throughout this chapter, that these writings accurately reflect Richardson's point of view, especially since they are consonant with the views expressed in his correspondence.

4. *The Richardson-Stinstra Correspondence and Stinstra's Prefaces to Clarissa*, ed. William C. Slattery (Carbondale: Southern Illinois University Press, 1969), p. 200. Hereafter cited as *Stinstra*.

5. *Amelia*, 3 vols. (Oxford: Blackwell, 1926), 3: 25–26. Another passage that suggests Harrison functions as the novel's, and perhaps the author's, spokesman is the following: "Of all mankind the doctor is the best of comforters. As his excessive good-nature makes him take vast delight in the office; so his great penetration into the human mind, joined to his great experience, renders him the most wonderful proficient in it; and he so well knows when to sooth, when to reason, and when to ridicule, that he never applies any of those arts improperly" (1: 111).

6. My examination of the trial of virtue in *Amelia* and *Clarissa* possibly invites comparison with R. F. Brissenden's basically thematic reading of *Clarissa* in *Virtue in Distress* (London: Macmillan, 1974), pp. 159–86. Perhaps surprisingly, Brissenden does not discuss *Amelia*.

7. Hunter, *Occasional Form*, p. 196.

8. Rothstein, *Systems of Order and Inquiry in Later Eighteenth-Century Fiction* (Berkeley and Los Angeles: University of California Press, 1975), pp. 157, 165; Rawson, *Henry Fielding*, p. 86; Hunter, *Occasional Form*, pp. 193, 209; Andrew Wright, *Henry Fielding, Mask and Feast* (Berkeley and Los Angeles: University of California Press, 1966), p. 50.

9. Elizabeth Bergen Brophy, *Samuel Richardson* (Knoxville: University of Tennessee Press, 1974), p. 94.

10. *Clarissa*, 8 vols. (Oxford: Blackwell, 1930), 1:66. I also wish to express my indebtedness to Shirley Van Marter, with whom I corresponded about the various editions of *Clarissa*, and from whose articles I learned a great deal. See especially, "Richardson's Revisions of *Clarissa* in the Second Edition," *Studies in Bibliography* 26 (1973): 107–32, and "Richardson's Revisions of *Clarissa* in the Third and Fourth Editions," *Studies in Bibliography* 28 (1975): 119–52.

11. Comparing the characters of Anna and Clarissa, Richardson himself

expresses some dismay about how they affected some contemporary readers. He writes: "I have often been surprized, that these two Characters have been very much mistaken by Persons of Taste, Virtue, Honour, who nevertheless have favoured the History with their particular Attention. Can it be, that to the one we know we are superior, and therefore are not Jealous?" (*SL*, p. 204).

12. Robert Alter, *Fielding and the Nature of the Novel* (Cambridge: Harvard University Press, 1968), p. 158; Kinkead-Weekes, *Samuel Richardson*, p. 161.

13. John Preston discusses the importance of attention in *The Created Self* (London: Heinenman, 1970), pp. 78–80.

14. Kinkead-Weekes, *Samuel Richardson*, p. 126; Eaves and Kimpel, *Samuel Richardson*, p. 280.

15. Morris Golden, *Richardson's Characters* (Ann Arbor: University of Michigan Press, 1963), p. 17; Margaret Anne Doody, *A Natural Passion* (Oxford: Clarendon Press, 1974), p. 124; Leo Braudy, "Penetration and Impenetrability in *Clarissa*," in *New Approaches to Eighteenth-Century Literature*, ed. Phillip Harth (New York: Columbia University Press, 1974), p. 205.

16. *The Rise of the Novel* (Berkeley and Los Angeles: University of California Press, 1974), p. 216.

17. Preston, *Created Self*, p. 61.

18. Alan Dugald McKillop, *Samuel Richardson, Printer and Novelist* (Chapel Hill: University of North Carolina Press, 1936), p. 170. McKillop further suggests that the "Concluding Note" to *Grandison*, where Richardson rejects "hasty reformation[s], introduced, in contradiction to all probability, for the sake of patching up what is called a happy ending," is directly aimed at Fielding (pp. 204–5).

19. See also Stinstra's wonderful discussion of poetic justice, *Stinstra*, pp. 194–205.

20. Rothstein, *Systems of Order and Inquiry*, p. 167; see also the discussion of the role of Providence in *Amelia* in Sheldon Sacks, *Fiction and the Shape of Belief* (Berkeley and Los Angeles: University of California Press, 1967), pp. 260–62.

Chapter 6

1. *The Yale Edition of the Works of Samuel Johnson*, vols. 3–5, *The Rambler*, ed. W. J. Bate and Albrecht B. Strauss (New Haven, Conn.: Yale University Press, 1963), 3:24. Subsequent volume and page citations in text refer to this edition (hereafter cited as *Rambler*).

2. *Lives of the English Poets*, ed. G. B. Hill, 3 vols. (Oxford: Clarendon Press, 1905), 1:170. Hereafter cited as *Lives*.

3. Leopold Damrosch, Jr., *The Uses of Johnson's Criticism* (Charlottesville: University of Virginia Press, 1976), p. 99.

4. Damrosch argues that Johnson's "postulate [in *Rambler 4*] is that art appeals to the imagination at an emotional level over which the intellect has only intermittent control" (p. 112). While the reader's emotional participation is certainly crucial, I also share William Edinger's view that "unlike most of his contemporaries Johnson repeatedly emphasizes the cognitive value of fiction"

(*Samuel Johnson and Poetic Style* [Chicago: University of Chicago Press, 1977], p. 99).

5. To an extent, some of what I have to say has been discussed in William Vesterman's essay, "Johnson and *The Life of Savage*," *ELH* 36 (December 1969): 659–78. For other recent examinations of the *Life of Savage*, see the following essays: John A. Dussinger, "Style and Intention in Johnson's *Life of Savage*," *ELH* 37 (December 1970): 564–80, which appears in altered form in Dussinger's book, *The Discourse of the Mind in Eighteenth-Century Fiction;* Paul K. Alkon, "The Intention and Reception of Johnson's *Life of Savage*," *Modern Philology* 72 (November 1974): 139–50; and Martin W. Maner, "Satire and Sympathy in Johnson's *Life of Savage*," *Genre* 8 (June 1975): 107–18.

6. Donald Greene, for example, has remarked about the *Life of Savage:* "In the brilliant psychologizing he put into it, he may have purged some of his own bitterness toward life"; and he later observes about the *Life:* "The greatness of the work lies in the amount of himself that Johnson put into it" (*Samuel Johnson* [New York: Twayne, 1970], pp. 29, 113). For an opposing view, which seems overstated, see Clarence Tracy, *The Artificial Bastard* (Cambridge, Mass.: Harvard University Press, 1953): "Johnson was strong precisely where Savage was weak: in prudence, common sense, and manly independence. But Savage fascinated him as a study in human behavior, as one of those 'modes of life' that Imlac was to find an essential part of a poet's knowledge" (p. 134).

7. *Life of Savage*, ed. Clarence Tracy (Oxford: Clarendon Press, 1971), p. xix. Hereafter cited as *Savage*.

8. Greene, *Samuel Johnson*, Preface, p. [9].

9. Paul Fussell, *Samuel Johnson and the Life of Writing* (New York: Harcourt Brace Jovanovich, 1971), p. 261.

10. Marshall Waingrow has dealt with the "symbolic force" of *The Life of Savage* in his unpublished essay, "Johnson's *Life of Savage:* Biography as Conjecture," that was read and distributed to MLA seminar 13 in Chicago, December 1973.

11. Sheldon Sacks, *Fiction and the Shape of Belief* (Berkeley and Los Angeles: University of California Press, 1967), pp. 26, 49. The works Sacks refers to by Bronson and Kolb are: Bertrand H. Bronson, ed., *Samuel Johnson: Rasselas, Poems, and Selected Prose* (New York: Rinehart, 1958), p. xvi; and Gwin J. Kolb, "The Structure of *Rasselas*," *PMLA* 66 (1951): 698–717. See also Carey McIntosh, *The Choice of Life* (New Haven, Conn.: Yale University Press, 1973), pp. 163–212.

12. This incontrovertible background is precisely formulated in Johnson's *Sermon XII*: "We may be content, at last, to conclude, that if happiness had been found, some would have found it, and that it is vain to search longer for what all have missed." This quotation is cited in James Gray, *Johnson's Sermons: A Study* (Oxford: Clarendon Press, 1972), p. 172.

13. This quotation is referred to in Chester F. Chapin, *The Religious Thought of Samuel Johnson* (Ann Arbor: University of Michigan Press, 1968), pp. 75–76.

14. Chapin, *Religious Thought*, p. 159.
15. Fussell, *Samuel Johnson*, pp. 217, 221, 224.
16. Arieh Sachs, *Passionate Intelligence* (Baltimore, Md.: Johns Hopkins University Press, 1967), p. 17.
17. W. K. Wimsatt, "In Praise of *Rasselas*: Four Notes (Converging)," collected in *Imagined Worlds*, ed. Maynard Mack and Ian Gregor (London: Methuen, 1968), pp. 111–36. The specific comments in this essay that I am responding to are, in order of quotation, on pages 128, 126–27, and 124.
18. *The History of Rasselas, Prince of Abissinia*, ed. Geoffrey Tillotson and Brian Jenkins (London: Oxford University Press, 1971), pp. 109–10. Hereafter cited as *Rasselas*.
19. Robert Voitle, *Samuel Johnson the Moralist* (Cambridge, Mass.: Harvard University Press, 1961), p. 135.
20. See *Rambler*, 3:223–24: "Almost all that we can be said to enjoy is past or future; the present is in perpetual motion, leaves us as soon as it arrives, ceases to be present before its presence is well perceived, and is only known to have existed by the effects which it leaves behind. The greatest part of our ideas arises, therefore, from the view before or behind us, and we are happy or miserable, according as we are affected by the survey of our life, or our prospect of future existence."

Chapter 7

1. Joseph Epes Brown, *The Critical Opinions of Samuel Johnson* (New York: Russel & Russel, 1961), p. 514.
2. *The Life and Opinions of Tristram Shandy, Gentleman*, ed. James Aiken Work (New York: Odyssey, 1940), 4:273. Hereafter cited as *TS*. See also Martin Battestin's brief reference to Sterne's "sixth sense" in *The Providence of Wit* (Oxford: Clarendon Press, 1974), p. 253.
3. See, for example, George Goodin's essay, "The Comic as a Critique of Reason: *Tristram Shandy*," *College English* 29 (December 1967): 215, where Goodin writes: "Tristram serves also to propound a view of reason which has become a twentieth-century commonplace in various forms such as Heisenberg's Uncertainty Principle. Stated very generally, this view of reason is that the measure or assessment of an 'object' is a function of the scale of values or perspective which is used to measure or assess with."
4. *The Letters of Laurence Sterne*, 2d ed., ed. Lewis Perry Curtis (Oxford: Clarendon Press, 1965), p. 411. Hereafter cited as *Letters*.
5. See especially Richard A. Lanham, *Tristram Shandy: The Games of Pleasure* (Berkeley and Los Angeles: University of California Press, 1973) and James E. Swearingen, *Reflexivity in "Tristram Shandy"* (New Haven, Conn.: Yale University Press, 1977).
6. Swearingen, *Reflexivity*, p. 12.
7. Traugott's remarks are included in a panel discussion collected in *The Winged Skull*, ed. Arthur H. Cash and John M. Stedmond (London: Methuen, 1971), p. 85.
8. Swearingen, *Reflexivity*, p. 6.

9. Gabriel Josipovici, *The World and the Book* (Stanford, Cal.: Stanford University Press,1971), pp. xiii–xiv. See also Helène Moglen, *The Philosophical Irony of Laurence Sterne* (Gainesville: University of Florida Press, 1975), pp. 147–62, where Professor Moglen briefly discusses Sterne's relationship to contemporary literature.

10. Howard Anderson, "*Tristram Shandy* and the Reader's Imagination," *PMLA* 86 (October 1971): 970.

11. William Freedman writes that in Tristram's history of the mind, "he takes it upon himself to make clear that past, present, and future, that events, emotions, and opinions all impinge upon one another as arbitrarily differentiated bands in the same experiential spectrum" ("*Tristram Shandy:* The Art of Literary Counterpoint," *Modern Language Quarterly* 32 [September 1971]: 272–73).

12. Lionel Trilling, "Art and Fortune," in *The American Novel since World War II*, ed. Marcus Klein (New York: Fawcett, 1969), p. 94.

13. Sigurd Burckhardt, "Tristram Shandy's Law of Gravity," *ELH* 28 (1961): 80–81.

14. Jean-Jacques Mayoux, "Variations on the Time-Sense in *Tristram Shandy*," in *Winged Skull*, ed. Cash and Stedmond, p. 3. See also Swearingen, *Reflexivity*, pp. 107–9.

15. Ian Watt, "The Comic Syntax of *Tristram Shandy*," in *Studies in Criticism and Aesthetics, 1660–1800*, ed. Howard Anderson and John S. Shea (Minneapolis: University of Minnesota Press, 1967), p. 320.

16. See William V. Holtz, *Image and Immortality: A Study of Tristram Shandy*, (Providence, R.I.: Brown University Press, 1970), pp. 80–89.

17. Swearingen, *Reflexivity*, p. 254.

18. *Biographia Literaria*, in *The Selected Poetry and Prose of Samuel Taylor Coleridge*, ed. Donald A. Stauffer (New York: Modern Library, 1951), p. 263.

19. Toby A. Olshin, "Genre and *Tristram Shandy*: The Novel of Quickness," *Genre* 4 (December 1971): 361.

20. Thomas Pynchon, *Gravity's Rainbow* (New York: Bantam, 1974), p. 3.

Chapter 8

1. See, for example, James T. Boulton, *The Language of Politics* (London: Routledge & Keagan Paul, 1963), pp. 226–32; David McCracken, "Godwin's *Caleb Williams*: A Fictional Rebuttal of Burke," *Studies in Burke and His Time* 11 (1969–70): 1442–52; and Gary Kelly, *The English Jacobin Novel, 1780–1805* (Oxford: Clarendon Press, 1976), pp. 179–208.

2. Here I am using the term melodrama in the specific sense in which Robert Heilman defines the term: "In the structure of melodrama, man is essentially 'whole'; this key word implies neither greatness nor moral perfection, but rather an absence of [a] basic inner conflict"; moreover, Heilman argues that the "emotional concomitants" of melodramatic structure are that "in one direction we are lured toward high confidence, in the other, toward

despair; in one direction toward self-glorification, in the other, toward feeling sorry for ourselves." *Tragedy and Melodrama* (Seattle: University of Washington Press, 1968), pp. 79, 87.

3. William Godwin, *The Enquirer* (New York: August M. Kelly, 1965), pp. 135, 136, 137, 139–40. Hereafter cited as *ENQ*.

4. *Caleb Williams*, intro George Sherburn (San Francisco: Rinehart, 1960), p. 4. Hereafter cited as *CW*.

5. D. Gilbert Dumas, "Things as They Were: The Original Ending of *Caleb Williams*," *Studies in English Literature 1500–1900* 6 (1966): 575–97.

6. The original conclusion is included as Appendix I of David McCracken's edition of *Caleb Williams* (London: Oxford University Press, 1970), pp. 327–34. Hereafter cited as *Appendix*.

7. Dumas, "Things as They Were," pp. 585, 593. On the other hand, the following recent articles do not succumb to melodramatic readings: Donald Roemer, "The Achievement of Godwin's 'Caleb Williams': The Proto-Byronic Squire Falkland," *Criticism* 18 (Winter 1976): 43–56; and C. R. Kropf, "*Caleb Williams* and the Attack on Romance," *Studies in the Novel* 7 (Spring 1976): 81–87.

8. William Hazlitt, *Complete Works of William Hazlitt*, ed. P. P. Howe, 21 vols. (London: Dent, 1932), 11:23.

9. Rudolf F. Storch, "Metaphors of Private Guilt and Social Rebellion in Godwin's *Caleb Williams*," *ELH* 34 (June 1967): 190, 192, 194. For other psychological approaches to *Caleb Williams*, see Robert Kiely, *The Romantic Novel in England* (Cambridge, Mass.: Harvard University Press, 1972), pp. 81–97; James Rieger, *The Mutiny Within* (New York: Braziller, 1967), pp. 34–48; and Christopher Small, *Ariel like a Harpy* (London: Victor Gollancz, 1972), pp. 68–99.

10. William Godwin, *Four Early Pamphlets* (1783–84), intro. Burton R. Pollin (Gainesville, Fla.: Scholars Facsimiles, 1966), p. 191.

11. See Eric Rothstein's excellent chapter on *Caleb Williams* in *Systems of Order and Inquiry in Later Eighteenth-Century Fiction* (Berkeley and Los Angeles: University of California Press, 1975), pp. 208–42.

Chapter 9

1. "'Nature' as Aesthetic Norm," in Arthur O. Lovejoy, *Essays in the History of Ideas* (New York: Putnam's, 1960), pp. 69–77. The reader should also consult the general discussions of nature in M. H. Abrams, *The Mirror and the Lamp* (New York: Norton, 1958), chapters 1 and 2, and in Walter Jackson Bate, *From Classic to Romantic* (New York: Harper, 1961), chapter 3. For specific discussions of the relation between Johnson's critical practice and his idea of nature, see Walter Jackson Bate, *The Achievement of Samuel Johnson* (New York: Oxford University Press, 1955), chapter 5; Jean Hagstrum, *Samuel Johnson's Literary Criticism* (Chicago: University of Chicago Press, 1967), chapter 4; R. D. Stock, *Samuel Johnson and Neoclassical Dramatic Theory* (Lincoln: University of Nebraska Press, 1973), chapter 2; and William Edinger, *Samuel Johnson and Poetic Style*, chapter 3.

2. R. G. Collingwood's *The Idea of Nature* (New York: Oxford University Press, 1965) is entirely devoted to how ideas of nature have changed.

3. See Richardson, *Selected Letters*, pp. 341–42.

4. R. G. Collingwood, *The Idea of History* (New York: Oxford University Press, 1974), p. 218.

5. Melvyn New, "'The Grease of God': The Form of Eighteenth-Century English Fiction," *PMLA* 91 (March 1976): 236.

6. Battestin, *The Providence of Wit* (Oxford: Clarendon Press, 1974), p. vii. For statements of views opposed to Battestin's providential readings, see Ronald Paulson's review of *The Providence of Wit* in *Studies in Burke and His Time* 17 (Autumn 1976): 234–40, and C. J. Rawson's review essay, "Order and Misrule: Eighteenth-Century Literature in the 1970's," *ELH* 42 (1975): 471–505.

7. Rothstein, *Systems of Order and Inquiry in Later Eighteenth-Century Fiction* (Berkeley and Los Angeles: University of California Press, 1975) pp. 2–3.

Index

Index

Fielding, Henry (*continued*):

Richardson, 3, 7, 71–72, 74, 79, 86–88, 89; compared with Defoe, 50. Works: *Amelia*, 7, 72–76, 79–80, 86, 88, 140; *Tom Jones*, 140
Freedman, William, 153 n.11
Free Thoughts on Religion (Mandeville), 28
Frye, Northrop, 1
Fussell, Paul, 95, 101

Gibbon, Edward, 10
Gildon, Charles, 50–51
Godwin, William: and tendency, 124–25, 131, 133–36. Works: *Caleb Williams*, 123–36, 140; *Enquirer*, 123–24, 136; *Enquiry Concerning Political Justice*, 123
Goodin, George, 152 n.3.
Greene, Donald, 95, 151 n.6
Gulliver's Travels (Swift), 10, 12, 13, 15–24, 28, 32, 37, 102

Hagstrum, Jean, 4
Harley, Robert, 48–49, 56
Harth, Phillip, 145 n.3, 146 n.13
Hayek, F. A., 146 n.14
Hazlitt, William, 135
Heilman, Robert, 153–54 n.2
Hirsch, E. D., 1
Hobbes, Thomas, 29
Homer, 3
Hopkins, Robert, 31
Horace, 3
Hume, Robert, 66
Hunter, J. Paul, 51, 75, 76

Idler 89 (Johnson), 96
Indeterminacy: in eighteenth-century fiction, 4–8, 140–42; and phenomenology of reading, 6–8; and Samuel Richardson, 71–72, 82, 88; and Samuel Johnson, 105–7, 108; and Laurence Sterne, 109–13, 118–19, 120–22
Iser, Wolfgang, 6

Jack, M. R., 31
Johnson, Samuel, 3, 51; and critical objectivity, 4; and affective criticism, 6–7, 90–93, 137–39; and equipoise, 96–99, 106–7, 108. Works: *Idler 89*, 96; *Life of Cowley*, 6; *Life of Milton*, 89–91, 138; *Life of Savage*, 89, 93–99, 102, 105, 106; *Life of Waller*, 91–92, 138; *Rambler 4*, 97, 99, 101, 107; *Rambler 60*, 5, 91, 92; *Rambler 70*, 96–97; *Rasselas*, 99–107; *Shakespeare*, 137, 138
Jonson, Ben, 3
Josipovici, Gabriel, 111
Journal of the Plague Year (Defoe), 54
Journey: Johnson's use of, 107; in eighteenth-century fiction, 114–15; Sterne's use of, 114–17
Juvenal, 3

Kimpel, Ben D., 82
Kinkead-Weekes, Mark, 79, 82

Latent fiction: and Swift's satire, 24; distinguished from manifest fiction, 30–31. *See also* Manifest fiction
Leavis, F. R., 9–11
Life of Cowley (Johnson), 6
Life of Milton (Johnson), 89–91, 138
Life of Savage (Johnson), 89, 93–99, 102, 105, 106
Life of Waller (Johnson), 91–92, 138
Longinus on aesthetic energy and invention, 3
Lovejoy, Arthur, 137

McCracken, David, 134
McKillop, Alan, 87, 150 n.18
Mandeville, Bernard, 13, 49, 73; satiric practice of, compared with Swift's, 30–33, 37, 45; and behavioral psychology, 31, 34–36, 43, 45, 147 n.18. Works: *Fable of the Bees*, 28–45; *Free Thoughts on Religion*, 28
Manifest fiction: in *Gulliver's Travels* and